Learn Faster, Smarter.

Accelerated learning strategies proven to improve your memory, increase your focus and limit distractions so that you can learn anything you want, whenever you want.

Magnus Granger

© Copyright 2020
All right reserved.

The work contained herein has been produced with the intent to provide relevant knowledge and information on the topic on the topic described in the title for entertainment purposes only. While the author has gone to every extent to furnish up to date and true information; no claims can be made as to its accuracy or validity as the author has made no claims to be an expert on this topic. Notwithstanding, the reader is asked to do their own research and consult any subject matter experts, they deem necessary to ensure the quality and accuracy of the material presented herein.

This statement is legally binding as deemed by the Committee of Publishers Association and the American Bar Association for the territory of the United States. Other jurisdictions may apply their own legal statutes. Any reproduction, transmission, or copying of this material contained in this work without the express written consent of the copyright holder shall be deemed as a copyright violation as per the current legislation in force on the date of publishing and the subsequent time thereafter. All additional works derived from this material may be claimed by the holder of this copyright.

The data, depictions, events, descriptions, and all other information forthwith are considered to be true, fair, and accurate unless the work is expressly described as a work of fiction. Regardless of the nature of this work, the Publisher is exempt from any responsibility of actions taken by the reader in conjunction with this work. The Publisher acknowledges that the reader acts of their own accord and releases the author and Publisher of any responsibility for the observance of tips, advice, counsel, strategies, and techniques that may be offered in this volume.

Table of Contents

Introduction
Chapter 1: Is the World Against You?
    The Flaw in IQ Tests
    Talent vs. Hard Work

Chapter 2: Getting Started
    The Power of Daily Affirmations
    Do Daily Affirmations Work?
    Motivate with Simple Words

Chapter 3: Four Ways to Get That Super Memory
    Method 1: Linking Method for Everyday Lists
    Method 2: Speed Reading for Cheating Surficial knowledge
        Pointing Method
        Tracking and Pacing
        The Scanning Method
        Incorporating the Skills of Speed Reading into Improving Memory
        How Speed Reading and Visual Memory Patterns Work Together

    Method 3: Fact Association
        Associate with Deep Examination
        BONUS: Using Acronyms and Acrostics

    Method 4: Mind Maps for Complex Matters
        Individual Vs. Group and Other Mind Mapping Possibilities
        The Benefits of Mind Maps
        What Do You Need to Start a Mind Map?

Chapter 4: Reel in That Focus

What Is Self-Discipline?
Building Self-Discipline
    Beginning the Day with Exercise
    Set Goals Each Day to Guide Your Progress
    Cut out Temptations
    Maintain a Steady Sleep Schedule (Even on the Weekends!)

Maintaining Your Self-Discipline
    Write Down Milestones and Track Your Progress
    Set Time for Fun

Self-Discipline Activities to Keep You Focused and Motivated
    Meditation for Self-Discipline
    The Pomodoro Technique

Chapter 5: Understanding Distractions and Knowing How to Overcome them

Six Tips to Eliminating Distractions
The Myth with Multitasking
Managing Addictions that Distract You

Chapter 6: Habits to Keep

Exercising the Body to Strengthen Learning
Exercising the Mind to Strengthen Learning
Eating to Support the Body and Mind
    Key Foods to Include in Your Diet
    Unhealthy Foods to Avoid for Improving Brain Health

Where to Now?
Resources

Introduction

Do you find it difficult to learn and remember information that you have read or received through instruction? Are you concerned about the impact of not retaining enough information to achieve a good understanding of the material for school or work? Finding the support that you need can be a challenge, especially when conventional standards of instruction are not working. As children, we may have experienced similar challenges in a school system designed to educate us in a one-fits-all system that doesn't work for everyone. Imagine spending the time and money on tutoring services, private instruction, specialized courses, and/ or other methods that make little progress in your education, then facing the same or similar struggles in adulthood. As a parent and teacher, I know exactly how you feel! I can identify with the frustration you are experiencing, as I have found that the way most of us are taught and the way we learn does not coincide with success. A good education requires investment, though financially, it can take a toll on our budget, especially when the results are lacking, and we struggle throughout the process. What if there was a way to bypass the unnecessary costs and lengthy tutoring sessions with a simple, effective plan to help you learn better and keep your progress on track?

A rigid and narrow-focused educational plan is not the best option for most of us, and yet many school curriculums use a standard model and have done so for years, from understanding everything, including mathematics, writing, and reading to science, history, and more. When we work to comprehend a specific lesson or an entire subject in general with some difficulty, how often have we been seen or categorized as 'in need of assistance', even while these needs are not always met adequately, whether this is provided in the form of a private tutor, or in the form of an enhanced learning program offered in some public schools. Often, what we think we lack is just poor educational methods that expect us to passively absorb information like a sponge. Even if this works for some of us, it is generally inefficient as most of us need engagement and interaction to understand and retain what we learn fully. As kids, we were subject to a school system that focused more on getting us 'caught up' with our peers, to digest each lesson on the same level. And as adults, this can also ring true. Anyone of any age can struggle with how information is presented before us

As a 54-year-old parent of two boys, I can say that I am well acquainted with how everyone learns differently. My situation is nothing new, and you may have experienced this yourself or have heard of these instances from friends or maybe colleagues. In a household of more than one child, there will always be one who is more academically inclined, and another not necessarily so. This environment can create healthy competition between the two at a young age, however, if left to fester, can quickly turn to unhealthy comparisons. I am guilty of not addressing this with my boys sooner, so I saw firsthand how quickly the loss of confidence in oneself can change someone so dramatically especially during one's teenage years. My younger boy was always comparing himself to his older, more 'smarter' brother, and this changed him from a bright, energetic child to someone who became withdrawn and quiet especially during family gatherings. Noticing this dramatic change, I knew that I needed to find a solution and I needed it fast! They say that 70% of a child's learning is done outside of school, so I knew that I couldn't just rely on the help of his teachers, I needed to be involved as much as I can to help my son find his confidence back.

How did I find the best practices and methods for teaching? I had lots of research to do! It felt like starting from scratch at first, though once I opened a few books and websites to read, it only became more interesting from then on. I was determined to help my son and other kids like him, excel in school, and make their way to college. If there were a lot of resources to learn from and help him along this path, I was excited to make this happen! Imagine seeing a child go from feeling unworthy and struggling with their education, to learning faster, and easily adapt to a new way of education that not only meets their educational needs but surpasses them!

Over the years, I took what I learned from working with my own son to start helping others just like him. I'd work to teach other people what they needed so that they could begin to learn to their potential. I recognized that though not everyone learns through conventional methods, we all can learn. I've worked with other children that needed that boost. I've worked with teenagers that were convinced that they'd never make anything of themselves because they were too 'slow', according to their teachers who simply didn't know how to reach them. I've worked with adults who wanted to better themselves as well. I believe that we do not all have to learn exactly the same way, and the diversity in how we all learn means that we have our own unique perspectives that we can take and that we can apply to the world we live in.

I can take you through this journey and give you the tools to help you succeed. Learning is a skill that you acquire, not something that you are born with. Every day, there are stories of people from all backgrounds and experiences, who benefit from learning a better way and can achieve goals they never imagined possible. You can learn at any age – don't let others dictate your learning path and potential!

Chapter 1: Is the World Against You?

Learning can be difficult and challenging at any age, and especially so if we believe that how we learn when we're younger continues into our adult years. When we are told that we have limitations set on our ability to learn, or that intelligence is set from birth, it can be discouraging and convinces us that what we can achieve in life is already predetermined. This has led to the idea that our entire capacity for learning, comprehension, and understanding as being defined before it is developed fully; and effectively, we allow ourselves to limit our own progress and ability with this way of thinking. Instead of seeing the limitless potential of our learning capacity, we've been conditioned to learn in a way where we absorb information passively, often by listening without engagement, when our brain craves for more stimulation and ways to become actively involved and mentally fit to digest, remember and apply information effectively.

There has been enough research to debunk the myth that we are either born a genius or at a level of intelligence that cannot be changed or expanded as we grow and learn. This unmasks the very truth that there are ways and methods in which we can learn faster and retain more information for longer periods of time. For a lot of us, we rely on adopting these skills early, often at school, where we spend the majority of our formative years learning and studying to discover our passion and dreams, before we step out into the 'real' world. But for those who struggle in the school environment, it can be difficult to realize that not every method taught and presented in this setting works for everyone.

When we learn, we often do so out of necessity to achieve good grades and advance further in life and our careers. As children and adults, we continuously learn to adapt to the world around us: evolving technology, new scientific studies and discoveries, and a constant change in world events. Whether we realize it or not, our brains are constantly absorbing new stimuli, and we can maximize our ability to remember, retrieve, and apply this information to our benefit. It is how we learn that makes a difference in how well we retain what we absorb. I began to realize that some of how we learn today is problematic for the following reasons:

One: The education system is generally passive. We are expected to listen and remember what we are told or taught, with little engagement or discussion involved. In a classroom setting, much of the material presented does not stick with us, because it isn't something we easily retain. Without engagement, memorizing information is not as effective, and retaining what we learn is even less successful. This will cause us to re-read and review material that we have been given to improve our knowledge, only to find that this method is ineffective. The amount of extra time spent to re-read material is of little use because it does not have staying power in our mind. This continues as we grow into adulthood, through workplace training and other methods that often mimic the classroom experience in childhood.

Two: The way we view reading and learning in general needs to change. Often, reading a book that is mandatory as part of a course or study material can feel forced or uninteresting. Once we establish a reason or a motivation to learn more about a subject, we can focus this energy and enthusiasm on giving merit to our study, thereby making the subject matter interesting and more retainable. Consider a subject you take a keen interest in, and how even with the challenge of learning about it, you'll continue to make every effort because of your desire to understand and learn it.

Three: Our minds are not regularly stimulated. Keeping our minds stimulated with new information is vital for neurogenesis. Neurogenesis is the formation of neural pathways in the brain, which provides more space and growth for retaining anything new that we learn. This is accomplished when we learn something new - a pathway is born, and with it, the potential for more knowledge and expansion of our capacity to retain and remember information. As a result, we can recall more and recall faster as we strengthen and further develop these pathways in such a way that it becomes easier to retrieve.

As I became familiar with my son's needs, it was clear that our existing education system was not allowing him to learn and absorb information effectively. When he tried to recall a specific date or event from history class, it was challenging because there was no incentive, nor an exciting element attached to what he was expected to learn. No amount of reading textbooks or reviewing lessons was working for my son. He grew less confident as the days went by and soon began to fear school, not for the fact that he did not think he could do well, but rather that he did not believe he had the ability to do well, so as to be able to change his circumstances around.

The Flaw in IQ Tests

Intelligence Quotient (IQ) is the standard way in which intellect is measured, with tests conducted for children often beginning at ages 10-12. These tests have been widely and popularly used as one of the primary methods of determining an individual's intelligence level. The IQ test assesses a person's performance overall based on their results from a series of exercises and puzzles, then compares these to other samples of people within the same age range. These tests are standardized and measure our cognitive ability, which is how our brain processes and utilizes information. This ability determines how quickly we can resolve an equation or problem that is set before us.

When we are made to do these tests, whether younger or later in life, we don't realize that not all factors are taken into consideration, such as one's attention span, memory, previously learned information, and how well we can retrieve what we already know. Since these factors are not included when these tests are administered and studied, it's unsurprising that we do not get a full a picture of our ability when it is being measured. For example, knowing certain facts and information beforehand is not part of the assessment.

This means that if you happen to know certain facts in advance, such as a historical period of time or specific scientific knowledge, you have an advantage over someone who have not been exposed to that kind of information beforehand, which may allow you to react quicker to resolving certain tasks or puzzles and achieve a better score.

Although this highlights how arbitrary test results can be, something else comes to forefront - the more information we learn and retain, the better equipped we are to score higher results on tests, which can lead to achieving more in life. This is especially the case if you've ever been in a job interview. In a job interview, having just slightly more knowledge over your competitor on a specific product or concept can be the ultimate deciding factor between being successful and unsuccessful.

This begs the question - are IQ tests good or bad for us? Do they measure a true and fair score of our learning capacity, or do they only measure what has been predetermined by others?

Like many, I considered IQ tests when reviewing my younger son's academic progress, who had consistently struggled to make good grades in school. After a series of tests, however, I noticed that he began to take to heart his scores, which were based on the knowledge and ability he had at the time that it was measured. Despite making improvements in some areas of his learning since he received those results, I noticed he became fixated on these scores, and ultimately allowed them to dictate what he could and couldn't do. When he couldn't solve a math problem for example, he would refer to his test results and say, "that's because I have low IQ." He hid behind these scores and felt comfortable with doing so.

Teachers also tend to rely on these scores when making an assessment of the students that they teach. An unconscious bias forms and this manifests in the time that they dedicate to their students. It is often the case that a student with the higher score will receive more attention and praise from their teachers, whereas those who land on the other end of the spectrum will have less of their time. Not only are these biases harmful for those who do not do well in those tests, much like my son, but it also forms a negative perception for others, as they would witness how clearly one's ability can be bound so strongly by whether their test score was high or low, regardless of the accuracy of the test results.

Talent vs. Hard Work

It's an age-old debate: talent vs. hard work. They say that hard work will never fail you so long as you put in the hard yards. But let's put forth a situation to consider:

Jake and George, two boys of the same age, have grown up together and have always been placed in the same class. Jake, a gifted child, with seemingly effortless high grades in all his classes has grown up familiar with receiving attention and praise for his academic results. George, on the other hand, struggles in all classes and can barely keep up with passing grades. Always exceeding his teachers' expectations, Jake is considered a genius. He displays confidence, and this already sets a good foundation for learning, which comes easily to him. Whilst George, despite putting a lot of effort into studying, finds that his grades often fall short of his goals. When teachers and other students consider the two, they automatically conclude that the boys' learning ability and intelligence is vastly different, and point to their respective results to confirm this judgement.

Teachers, parents, and society, in general, will tend to focus their energy on Jake, as they see him as having unlimited potential for success, while George fades into the background, with no one paying any particular attention to him and his efforts. However, George firm on his belief that he will excel, decides to study twice as hard and twice as much in order to improve his grades. His studying methods are an extension of what he's been taught at school that have been ineffective thus far. But George has little choice, as he does not have the attention from his teachers, as his teachers have since decided that with his low test scores, he simply could not improve. They believe that his time would be better placed focusing on developing his vocational skills as clearly academics is not his forte and try to convince him of such. Jake on the other hand finds that every time he requires help, the people around him are available. This means that even if there are times when he slacks off, he has the support around him to make up for it. Jake is recommended for a career in science or medicine, which he also believes is the natural path to take.

If we stop to assess the two, it is clear that Jake has everything set up for success, whereas George has all the odds stacked against him. You may have found yourself in a similar situation where progress seems an uphill battle, and it's you against the world. And so, you would know that George's efforts alone do not get him to where he would like to be, despite how much of an underdog success story we'd all like to see.

They say that continuously doing the same thing the same way, only to hope for a different result is the definition of insanity. Hard work by repeating the same methods of learning that don't work, are wasted efforts. If our goal is to level the playing field with those whom society deems as infinitely more talented, we must think differently to how we're used to. For George, belief and hard work are simply not enough, as what he must first change is the way he has been learning for him to excel.

Rest assured, there are ways to circumvent the road to success. And here, I will show you the simple strategies that will allow you to do so. Let's begin!

Chapter 2: Getting Started

When we seek to make changes in our lives, we must first recognize what it is that needs changing. Improving your memory, retaining information, and learning more effectively all begins with setting a positive mindset. This may seem quite simple or easy, but the habitual nature of how we see our own potential and the way we have approached the learning process, will make it difficult. Some practices we may consider beneficial for learning may be working against us because we shape what we learn by what we already know, what we think we know or understand, and our perceived potential for learning. So, to establish a better way of learning and retaining information, we first have to change our mindset and how we view the way we acquire and retain information that we have adopted so far in school, work, and life.

First, we must forget about what you know or think you know, because it hasn't worked. The passive, listen-and-memorize approach, which is used in many formats of teaching, is simply not working. There are other ways to learn better that we must discover, which will allow us to rewrite the learning process. We must seek methods that allows for creativity and innovation so that our minds are engaged and learning itself can be an enjoyable process.

What we already know can work against us, and this is because we subconsciously limit new information about a topic when we consider our knowledge about it to be superior. When this happens, we override our ability to absorb new findings, which is often more relevant and accurate. This is especially true for scientific research, current news events, and discoveries that uncover history and information. Letting go of what we know is imperative to embracing new facts, which may or may not coincide or 'fit' into our previous knowledge. It is important to be flexible and open our minds to the possibility of change.

When our minds are open to learning, we have a better chance of retaining more than we think. This level of openness or engagement is expanded when we move into a transfixed or level of focus, as we would during a suspenseful movie or film, which holds our attention captive, and virtually nothing can disrupt our fixation. When we shift our minds into this state, we become more receptive to learning and absorbing information. It also becomes effortless, as we move into this state of believing and receiving new information, because we are not limited by social and preconceived constructs about what we are capable or not capable of.

When I started, I set out to make my son understand the implications of how we learn and how much our perceived abilities can impact how well we perform. It took some convincing, but once he understood it, I noticed an expression of relief on his face. It was a defining moment, as he realized that his success and ability to learn and improve his memory was not defined by any tests or conclusions drawn from them. It was a pivotal moment when we both understood how his potential could be 'unlocked', like a secret level in a puzzle or online game, taking us further. Not only did this realization help improve my son's confidence and determination to improve his memory and learning, but it also gave him a sense of power and control over himself to achieve beyond what he was told he could accomplish. We created a plan to work towards helpful practices that would allow him to 'rewire' his approach to learning.

One of the most important aspects of learning is self-awareness. How well do you retain information after reading a chapter in a book? Do you find yourself re-reading one or more paragraphs or chapters to understand them better? This is a struggle with many as we are not often aware of how well they absorb and retain new facts. This occurs because we are distracted and not fully open to taking in all the information presented to us, and it can seem overwhelming, even when it isn't. This was the case with my son, who was often distracted by his phone or a show on television, from the next room. Many of us are similarly impacted by distractions and how other people view us impact our sense of self-worth. While minimizing distractions and removing devices during studying was helpful, my son continued to struggle with focus, so we took it a step further with meditation. Focusing on the present is one of the best tools for avoiding or tuning out 'noise' that can interfere with our progress.

Being in the present and forgetting about past failures and possible future mistakes is the key to giving your learning experience the full potential you deserve. We started with meditation for just 10 minutes each day, then progressed longer, to 15-20 minutes. My son and I would practice together, in a quiet space outdoors or inside. Sometimes with soft music or soundscapes. Breathing deep, measured breaths helped him establish focus, and opened his mind to embrace new information. Quite quickly were we able to see results - he was able to read lessons and remember them much better than before, simply because his mind was unattached to any barriers or restrictions. This was a major step in improving focus and retention, both of which helped him to retrieve later, in class, and during exams, and as a result, his grades began to improve. You will find this method not only calming and better for sharpening your attention span, but it will also give you better quality for absorbing and learning information that is not easily interrupted. This is how studying works best: if you focus your mind and release the tension and stress of the day, you'll begin to see results within a short time!

Before you can work on techniques for improving memory and learning skills, setting a strong foundation with an open mind, a fresh approach to new information, and letting go of your past, is imperative. All of this is easy to achieve when your confidence is improved. This will happen when you realize how this connects to your ability to learn. Daily affirmations are an effective way to begin the process of feeling better about yourself and your abilities. At first, I was skeptical because the notion of using statements to establish self-esteem seemed contrary to what we often do internally, which is to listen to that voice that constantly tells us what we can't do. Negative self-statements are common, and we often hear them inside when they are most destructive, such as "you can't pass that exam" or "you're not good enough to get that promotion." These are self-defeating, and while affirmations may seem too easy to work, consider some promising studies from people who have successfully used them to improve their outlook on themselves and their abilities. Before you can put self-affirmations to the test, banish your negative thoughts and rebuild your inner voice with "I can," "I am capable," and "I deserve this". The power of positivity is rewarding when put into action.

The Power of Daily Affirmations

Positivity has everything to do with how well we perform and our success in life. How we approach each task and goal depends largely on how we view ourselves, which is often critical. In some cases, we might become so negative that we only hear self-deprecating comments from the voice in our head, which echoes criticisms we may have endured from others' opinions and feedback. Even when someone provides constructive criticism, we may not always take it as an opportunity for growth and improvement, even if it was the original intention. While constructive feedback is important, it is often too easy to become absorbed in negative thoughts and ideas about our self- worth and potential. Daily affirmations are an excellent tool to combat negative emotions and feelings about yourself while recharging your self-esteem and reestablishing your direction towards achievement.

When you begin using daily affirmations, or positive statements that improve your self-esteem, it will take some practice. Start with simple statements first, to get used to this practice. We've been subjected to negative, limiting statements about our learning since young, that it'll take time for these behaviors to be undone. Consider changing the nature of each statement such as the below:

- Change "I'm not good at writing" to "I'm capable of learning and improving how I write"

- Switch "I can't do this project" to "I have the ability and tools to complete and excel in this project"

The key to changing your negative thinking to positive affirmations is switching what you 'can't' do with your ability to learn and progress. You don't have to be perfect, or see yourself as such; instead, see you. And, combining this with meditation, this works extremely well, by opening your mind and learning potential to 'talking' yourself into a confident frame of mind to advance yourself further. As children, our success is often measured against our siblings and/or peers and we tend to forget to refocus on our own merits and abilities. This continues when we are older, too, as we compare our achievements or what we think we lack against colleagues and friends. By opening your mind to embracing a wider range of potential, you can achieve more with the benefits of meditation and daily affirmations. In working with my son and other children, I began to see a marked improvement in assignments within just a few weeks. Similarly, you will begin to see marked improvements in your understanding of concepts and modules of study for upgrading your skills for school or work.

If you are new to daily affirmations, as my son and I were, think of some empowering, simple statements that work for you and fit within your goals. Try two or three every day, and change them up, as new statements become more effective for various goals and projects. The overall goal is to improve our sense of self and become more aware of how we view ourselves. When my son and I began using daily affirmations, he was a bit hesitant and skeptical, finding the idea of 'talking' to himself as 'lame' as kids his age called it. However, once we tried one, then two statements, I noticed a significant shift in his disposition. He began to take affirmations seriously, and within a few days, practiced them on his own. In a short time, he was able to shed many of the negative feelings he felt towards himself, from comparing his grades and abilities to that of his older brother or his peers. It became a competition within himself, to try and excel to achieve his own very best. Once you hear yourself say something positive about you, even for the first time, it has a powerful effect immediately. It was amazing to see how empowering these affirmations were for my son and satisfying to witness, firsthand, their impact on his progress.

Try a few below, as they have helped my son immensely.

"I am worthy of praise and respect." This is a powerful and commanding line that reinforces your worthiness of being treated with respect and dignity. It is especially important if you have suffered from low self-esteem and difficulty standing up for yourself. This affirmation will allow yourself the permission to stand up and tolerate nothing less than respect. It is also a reminder that we must also respect ourselves to improve our confidence and positive thinking.

"I can do this!" This is great to start off any day, as it is simple but effective. This statement can give you the boost you need to take charge every day and make a difference. If you are a bit apprehensive about trying

affirmations, practice until you feel comfortable, and don't feel bashful about using them often. The more we hear ourselves say something positive, the better we feel inside.

"I'm in charge of my destiny." We can't control how everyone sees or perceives who we are, but we can make positive changes once we realize how much capacity we have. There are no limits, and we are all in control of our life and success. Your destiny is for you to determine, and once you realize this, you will feel overwhelming motivation to learn and retain more. Success is ultimately in your hands.

"I know I can accomplish anything I put my mind to." This is a great one to boost your morale and reassure yourself that you can get anything done that you set your mind to. It's also an excellent way to improve confidence, especially if you are preparing to study for a final exam or difficult project. Don't let others determine your ability. You know yourself better than anyone and focusing your mind on achieving your goals is a major step towards success.

"I have the skills to succeed." You have a valuable set of skills within, and no test score or perception can change this. Focus on what you can do, not what you think your limits are, and focus on developing your skills and making them work for you.

"I can improve." No one is perfect, and while many of us are hard on ourselves when we don't live up to our expectations (or others), we forget to notice that others are watching, whether it's our family, children, colleagues, and people we interact with regularly. They may hear all the positive reinforcement and encouragement we give them while noticing our own struggle with self-esteem. When this happens, take it on the chin and acknowledge it, but make a promise to yourself that you will treat *you* better. We all can make improvements, and sometimes the smallest changes are the best, because they will shift our direction in a more positive way of thinking and learning.

Do Daily Affirmations Work?

Is there proof behind positive comments and statements? Do they have any real meaning and power? You'd be glad to know that research have supported this, confirming that positive reinforcements make a significant impact on benefiting one's self-esteem. By applying positive affirmations in practice, you'll find that the words linger in your mind, and have a lasting effect over time. We use them to motivate ourselves into action and develop healthy patterns subconsciously over time. Late 19th and early 20th century findings from leading psychologists suggests that the reasons why these positive, reinforcing phrases work include the following:

- The consistency of making daily affirmations a part of your life has empirically improved how we see ourselves while helping to maintain self-integrity. We learn that we "owe it to ourselves" to feel good about who we are, and this increases confidence

- Daily affirmations reinforce our ability to protect our own best interests and self-esteem from harm. In other words, you are more likely to stand your ground and speak better of yourself than without them. When a person or situation threatens your confidence, you're more likely to brush off the negativity and not allow the threatening nature of this behavior to impact you as much

- Keeping the narrative in your head positive will dismantle all the unkind words and thoughts that replay in our minds. These negative thoughts occur when we hear them from other people. Long after we think that those comments have disappeared, they can resurface later in a pattern of put-downs and self-deprecating comments that are counterproductive. Daily affirmations effectively reverse the damage of negativity and boost our self-esteem to a better level

- Writing daily affirmations in colorful letters and placing them in a comfortable area as a reminder is also wonderfully powerful in giving you that extra reminder. There will be days when you skip the self-affirming phrases because you are too busy or have other plans that require a change in schedule. When this happens, visual affirmations that can pop out at you every morning act as a reminder that we deserve to feel good about who we are.

Self-affirmation theory states that we can change the course of negativity, even long-term lack of self-esteem into a positive, motivating outlook that will effectively build our sense of worthiness. Other aspects of your life will also be improved, as you will find that you will be better equipped to adapt to various situations and handling difficulties in life. Daily affirmations directly impact not only the way we see ourselves but also how we behave and react when confronted with a challenge.

So, what are the advantages of these positive statements, according to this science?

- When you use self-affirming statements, the level of stress is reduced. This is supported by studies involving people who applied daily affirmations as a means to reinforce confidence. It has a soothing effect on your mind, and by speaking in a kind and compassionate tone of voice, you'll be able to calm your mind, which decreases stress as well

- Daily affirmations can help reduce the likelihood that we will take constructive criticism or interventions the wrong way. This is because we will be less defensive and less likely to assume the worst-case scenarios

- The more satisfied you are with yourself, the more apt you are to eat better and make healthier and sound decisions in your choice of food. That is, self-affirmations and feeling good about yourself translate into improved eating choices, such as eating more fruits and vegetables

- One of the most amazing effects of daily affirmations is the ability to increase academic performance and outcomes. The better you feel about yourself, the more likely you will achieve higher grades and perform well overall

- Lower stress and healthier choices due to self-affirmations have been noticed along with better physical activity and performance as well, which means you are more likely to exercise and perform better when doing so, as a result of reinforcing a better perception of yourself.

By introducing and maintaining the practice of daily affirmations, not only are we improving our state of mind and achievements, but we can also heal and improve from the damage caused in the past from negative emotions and lack of positive results. For many of us, even in childhood, we are accustomed to thinking that we need to do better, or that what we do must improve. Sometimes it's benign thoughts we conjure up from comparing ourselves to people on television, celebrities, or other people we know in school and through family who are labeled as high achievers. Remember those people who could do no wrong, and who were held to a high standard as the ultimate way to achieve and be? As kids, some of us may have been compared to them. I've seen this happen with some of the children I've worked with to improve self-esteem and learning habits. This can be detrimental to a degree because most of us are already critical of ourselves, and this only perpetuates the negativity. We may not realize the impact of self-comparison, and this can have long-term effects, stretching into our adulthood. Once we discover that what we can do is beyond our expectations and we do not have the restrictions we think we have, then we can make a difference.

Motivate with Simple Words

What if you are uncomfortable with the idea of using daily affirmations? Is there a way to introduce the process gently to stir enthusiasm? Some of you may find it challenging at first, so it's best to begin with words that are simple. Consider some of the uplifting and encouraging statements you would have wanted to hear as a child, then convert them into what will help you now. You'll be surprised to notice many of these statements remain the same, as we often carry our struggles with us into adulthood. In one of my discussions with my son, I came up with a list of words and asked him to start applying his own meaning to them. It is important that you provide your own understanding to words whose meanings are seemingly obvious. Once you unpack what these words mean to you, you'll be able to focus on how you feel within to start building a foundation to achieve the successes you lay out.

Happiness

Are you happy? Do you help others feel happy? Take a step back and have a think about what ultimately makes you happy and what that looks like. Does it involve comparing yourself with others, or do you just want to be happy with what you have and who you are? For some people, feeling happy about themselves can signal a self-esteem challenge. But chances are, despite having challenges in life, you will still be able to find something that makes you happy or content. Focus on this and make it a focal part of your life. This will help improve the motivation to achieve greater happiness by achieving the goals you want to accomplish.

Forgiveness

We all make mistakes and can be hard on ourselves for them. If we make every effort to correct a wrong action or statement made to someone, it'll be a never-ending cycle of self-loathing. We are only human, and we can only do our best. We may or may not receive forgiveness from someone else, so we must forgive ourselves first. Forgiving others is a practice used to find and make peace, even in situations where the other person doesn't show remorse or that they are sorry for something said or done. Once we forgive ourselves, it is a liberating experience: we no longer feel trapped by our mistake(s) and can move onto a positive solution and path. "I will forgive myself and make positive change," and "I deserve to be forgiven." Both statements are powerful ways of moving forward to a better mindset and being proactive.

Growth

As we grow into adulthood, we learn much along the way, right through to our adult years. As a middle-aged parent, I continue to learn new and innovative ways to help my children and myself develop skills. Without continual growth and learning, we become stagnant and will not improve upon what we already know. Some people may not realize their potential and shy away from methods that could improve much about their life. Permit yourself to improve. "I can improve, grow, and develop," is a powerful phrase to keep in your roster of daily affirmations. This is a part of your personal growth and evolution into achieving more and better each time.

Solutions

Where there is a problem, you'll find the solution. This does not mean it will always be easy, but sometimes the way to fix a problem can be unusual or haven't been considered before. This is where the term 'thinking outside of the box' applies in many situations. "I can and will find a solution," and "I am capable of resolving a problem" may seem simple, but they are effective, especially if you need that reassurance. Some problems may take longer to resolve than others, which is why it's important to see yourself as a part of the solution, and soldier on even when you hit obstacles.

Improvement

"I will get better each day" and "I can improve more every day" are great examples of helping to understand the power of positive thinking. Even if you do not think you can resolve a problem, it's important to realize that you have the power to improve. Everyone can get better over time. It takes confidence and a willingness to learn and progress. Reassuring yourself that you can make a difference by applying what you already know and learning more, you'll be able to see that you are capable of great achievements.

Leader

Often, we are the first to dismiss ourselves as leaders and lean on others to lead us, even if we can be just as capable. "I can lead" or "I am a leader" may seem like a stretch for some, who may be embarrassed with the idea of taking charge, but leading can actually take on many forms. For example, you can lead by example and help others to achieve their goals in school and later at work or within the community. Establishing a sense of self-awareness and duty is important. While this means more responsibility, it is important to allow yourself to embrace this as a powerful tool for achieving more with others.

Have a think about your own meaningful words and allow yourself to be reminded of them when you hit that figurative roadblock. You will find that they'll become your compass to anchor you should you hit any type of setback on this learning journey.

Now that you have a changed mindset and a positive outlook, you are now primed to take on the effective methods that will change your learning journey.

Chapter 3: Four Ways to Get That Super Memory

Memory is the most important thing to how we learn. The more information you can retain, the more prepared you will be when you are put to the test, both literally and figuratively. Improving your memory isn't just repeating concepts and facts in your mind over and over again. Whilst rote learning can have its positive effects with simple things like the multiplication table in Math, it isn't as effective with more complex ideas and the ever-changing situation of life. Not to mention, it also isn't the most fun and inspiring way to learn.

In working with my son, I researched several methods to improve my son's memory. These techniques produced effective results over time and allowed him to not only successfully achieve the academic goals he set out for himself, but more importantly allowed him to enjoy the *process* of learning. When we learn and retain new facts, concepts, and put them into practice, this mental exercise allows you to build stronger thinking and learning skills. By applying these techniques into our everyday life, not only will we see an improvement in our ability to remember more and accurate information, we'll see better test results, and recall what we've learned more readily, like having an encyclopedia or reference guide in our mind.

Method 1: Linking Method for Everyday Lists

The linking method of learning and memorizing information is a simple concept that can help you retain more information and will better accuracy. This is done by effectively 'linking' or connecting an image or relatable concept with an item or list of items that you are learning. For example, you can associate certain images or colors with various concepts or to a list of items that you may have difficulty remembering. By making a connection in your mind with a familiar, identifiable object associated with that list, you will not only remember the item(s) but can visualize them in your mind vividly and interpret and apply them more effectively as a result. This exercise is especially effective and fun for those visual learners who struggle with the traditional listen-and-repeat model.

Step One

Consider a list of items, names, dates, and/or places that you must remember as a part of a lesson or learning material. Often, these items on the list may seem abstract or 'dry' and difficult to memorize because they have no relevance or connection to anything in your personal life, and as a result, are difficult to relate to and remember. Consider associating the list of these items with various colors or images, starting with the first item. This may be a person's name, a location, or a color that you can associate with the first listed item. Across from the list of items you wish to memorize, write a second list that connects each item to a secondary list of items that you can relate to, such as visuals or pictures that you can easily create or conjure in your mind.

Step Two

As you review each item on the list you wish to memorize, starting with the first item, then second, third, fourth, and so on, you'll have a relatable or 'attached' secondary list that correlates each item you need to remember with a memorable image that is now imprinted into your mind. This secures the way you will remember the list, not only to memorize each item but the order in which they are presented. This is especially useful if you are trying to remember a list of chronological dates.

Try this method with every list or group of items you wish to remember and consider how they can connect with an easier set of items that you have difficulty recalling. This relatable or linking method is effective, even if it seems bizarre or unusual at first. You don't have to 'link' or connect items that have relevance that other people recognize, as long as they work for you. For example, if you have the word 'pirate' on your list, the color 'blue' may resonate with this term due to the color of the sea or the ocean; or, it may simply be the first color you think of when pirates come to mind. Either way, if it is effective, go ahead and use it!

How do you apply this method to the everyday? A shopping list is an excellent example of how this works. For your next trip to the grocers, consider using this exercise to help recall a simple list of items to buy. How often do you head to the grocers to get a small list of items, only to forget at least of the items by the time you reach home? By visualizing your list of items together, you can make it easier to remember which items you need, without worrying about missing one or two. Consider the following methods for building your visual, memorable list that you can take with you on your next trip:

On a recent shopping trip with my son, I recorded the following list of grocery items I needed at the supermarket:

- Chicken breast
- Tomato sauce
- Yogurt

- Spices (listed separately or simply as 'spices')
- Cucumber
- Cooking oil

In reviewing these items, ask yourself - what do they have in common, and why do they need to be purchased together? One clue is this: they are a part of a common goal, such as a recipe, which may be easy to recall once you visualize all the items on the list that are used to make it. When I asked my son what all the items had in common, he tried to imagine a picture in his mind with all the ingredients, then focused on how they would interact with one another: would the tomatoes be coated in spices, then sliced and layered over the chicken? This idea would essentially take care of half the list already! The remaining items could be combined with sliced cucumbers over a bowl of yogurt, next to the chicken breast covered in tomato, spices, and olive oil. If this is the case, consider labelling this list as the name of a recipe in your mind: spicy tomato marinated chicken, for example, and use this option to remember these items, so that half the ingredients are already remembered for you the next time you head out to the shops. The following week, we expanded the list to add two more items, which prompted my son to imagine another scenario, to incorporate the additional foods. In recalling the list and gradually expanding and/or changing the items on the list from one week to the next, he was able to recall longer lists effectively and effortlessly.

When all the ingredients on your grocery list do not create a recipe, you will need to get a bit creative, if you want to visualize your list! This is where my son used his creative skills to paint an image in his mind of something new and exciting. If the items do not 'fit' together, you can create a fun 'story' or visual instead. Imagine the grocery list consists of items that are not related in any way and may not be as simple to recall once you need to remember them on a whim. What you need to do instead is think about how each of these items can be remembered as a visual interpretation in your mind:

- Apples
- Yogurt

- Salmon
- Frozen entrees
- Potatoes
- Vinegar
- Sea salt

In the above list, there are no recipes or common denominator to group these items into an easy-to-remember list, which means you'll want to get a bit more creative in how you remember them. To imagine how this can be done, try visualizing the following items in the following way:

- Imagine a large bowl of yogurt with apples slowly 'raining' or descending into it, which covers the first two items on your list

- In the second visual, imagine the salmon 'swimming' through a maze of frozen entrees, as they navigate towards the bowl of yogurt and apples. These images already include four or nearly half of the contents included on your grocery list

- Continue this exercise by imagining another fun, even silly visual, for example of potatoes marching into a river of vinegar, where it is raining sea salt. This now covers your entire list!

This method works well because it is fun and can sometimes take away the monotony from your day. With a bit of creativity, you can imagine a colorful story with all the items woven together into motion instead of memorizing all the items on your list individually. You have now created a funny and graphic visual of how these foods move and react to one another in a series of mental animations or 'stories'. Repeat these three visuals in your mind to get a sense of all the seven items included. Instead of fixating on each item individually in your mind, you can create a collection of objects strewn into a visual or set of pictures that can help you remember. If you can attach significance to several images in a specific order, for example, one emerging from another, this is another way to improve the flow of visuals in your mind and help you to remember. For example, if you imagine one item of the list falling and landing into a basket, followed by another food or item, then a third, fourth, and so on, this layered effect can make it easier for you to recall the list. You will be able to recall not only which foods or objects to include, but also within a certain order, or an order that may be important in the bigger scheme of things.

In my experience working with children and adults alike with these visuals, I've seen great improvements within a short period. It also helps that they become more engaged and excited about how they can recall more items than before, and often in a specific order as well. It's a great way to instill confidence and a sense of achievement, and it is fantastic for those who have a more visually oriented mind. Imagine applying the same method to a list of words, concepts, or phrases that must be remembered for an upcoming quiz or test, or of everything that you need to remember for the next coffee run that you are tasked with picking up at work. This can also apply to learning a new language or a list of new terms that pertain to a specific subject, such as in science or history. Geography is another good example, as it can be challenging for some people to remember the capital of every state or where certain countries are located on a map. Visualization works wonders for these tasks and makes memorizing easy because you automatically paint a picture in your mind of these objects and their connection or association with each other.

Consider the following example I worked on with one of my older clients, who was learning Spanish. Each week, his teacher would provide a list of 10-12 new words to learn, which are required to be committed to memory and used in sentences. My client would become stressed towards the end of the week when the teacher would hand out a quiz asking for each of the words to be translated or used in a sentence. The task itself may seem easy enough, though with many other subjects to study and other lessons to commit to memory, this weekly list became a burden. There were no guides to learn the words either: the list could be comprised of terms that could relate to one another or, not; or they could be nouns, verbs, and adjectives. Practice assignments were helpful, but they did little to create associations between the words and their relevance. Also, each weekly list of words would be partially implemented in future lessons, even if the students didn't quite understand or become familiar with them. It felt as though each week's new list of words were simply dumped or added to the pile already required to be studied by the students. There was little room for questionings or not knowing how to use a word. To remedy this approach, which did not seem to be working effectively, we began to make our associations and visuals to better learn and understand each list. Here is an example of a weekly list distributed to the students in his class (the words below were given in another language originally – verbs in other languages are often one word, even when not conjugated):

- Dog
- Pet food

- To care for (verb)
- House
- Garden
- To walk (verb)
- To sleep (verb)
- Recreational
- Happy
- Playful
- Funny
- To cook (verb)

Consider the above list and imagine committing this to memory, along with the translation into another language, such as Spanish, French, or another popular language for students. How quickly can you remember these words on their own, not to mention their respective translations? The list includes verbs, adjectives, and nouns. As part of learning this list, you'll also need to conjugate the verbs. Conjugating verbs means changing the root form or version of the verb 'to sleep', for example, to fit a specific pronoun, such as 'I sleep', 'you sleep', 'they sleep', etc. This also pertains to other tenses, such as past tense, 'I slept' or the future 'I will/am going to sleep'. Simply memorizing these words can be a challenging task, even without the translations and various forms of each verb, especially if they are given no context. One of the best methods I used to help remember and apply words is by writing a story, even a few sentences, to create a common thread or connection:

> *My dog loves going out to walk in the mornings because he is playful and enjoys the park. I always feed him before we go outside. We enjoy the garden, and the recreational park makes him happy because there is a lot of space. I like to cook for him sometimes, instead of feeding him pet food, and I let him eat in the house. When he is tired, my dog enjoys a good sleep. I love to care for him because he is a part of my family. He is also funny and a great friend.*

The above sentences can be shortened or modified to make them easier to follow and remember. One major advantage of incorporating all the words in the list in the one paragraph or story is that you are able to create an association of all the words. Some people may not automatically associate 'to cook' or 'to sleep' with caring for a dog, but with the above, these can easily be fit into the story. To further enhance the success of learning these words, consider the visualizing the story, and animate it in your mind: imagine your pet dog playing in the park, then bringing him inside for a snack while you cook some food, and so on. The order of events can be changed to make it fun and easy. The order of the words can also be switched, even categorized. At first, you may want to organize the list according to word type, as follows:

Nouns:

- Dog
- Pet food
- House
- Garden

Adjectives (may also be used as nouns, depending on context):

- Recreational
- Playful
- Happy
- Funny

Verbs:

- To care for
- To walk
- To sleep
- To cook

This method of categorizing each group of words will work well for you if you need to concentrate on conjugating verbs, or if you are learning how to apply adjectives in a sentence, and/or definite (and indefinite) articles for nouns, which vary from one language and word to another. You may find both the visualizing process and the grouping of words in their respective categories helpful for tests and exams, which require words to be used and applied in various ways. Ultimately, the goal is to focus on learning the language enough to communicate effectively, and eventually, increasing your fluency as well.

Method 2: Speed Reading for Cheating Surficial knowledge

On average, we are able to read between 250-300 words per minute. As we read, we absorb each word, and its meaning, fully vocalizing or 'hearing' them in our minds as we articulate the sentences and paragraphs that make up the article or story. This speed, however, doesn't maintain itself and like many things, it is only when you keep at it that you're able to sustain it. When reading this book, what do you think your word per minute being read is?

Improving the speed at which we read doesn't just allow us to 'finish the book quicker', though that's quite obvious. Speed reading allows you to exercise and enhance your brain's capacity to improve on your memory, and this allows you to train your mind to its maximum potential. Speed reading increases the amount we comprehend by allowing your mind to take a few shortcuts along the way. Instead of reading or viewing each word on own, we can 'sub-vocalize' or broaden our view of each word or groups of words into phrases and sentences, which allow you to not only progress faster, but understand just as well as you would if absorbing each word at a time. This faster method makes it easier to put words into context quickly, as they are combined with others in sentences and paragraphs. There are several ways to learn speed reading, which can help you absorb more material within a shorter period of time.

Pointing Method

This has been a popular method to increase the number of words you can read and absorb within a short period. Some research has claimed that by using one's finger or a card as a guide to reading each line, you are able to increase your reading speed up to ten times. This is because each line or section is highlighted in such a way that you can focus clearly and quickly, then move on to the next phrase. When one sentence or line is highlighted or underlined with a card or alternate guide, it allows your brain to focus solely on it, with the ability to move forward onto the next line, and so on. If you find that you have difficulty focusing on reading, this is an ideal way to 'point' or direct your attention to the relevant sentence or line, then quickly moving to the next, and so on. A ruler, card, or any device that effectively underlines each line will work.

Tracking and Pacing

This method works much like the pointing method, only it focuses on one sentence at a time, using a pen. This is a great option for those who need to read more volumes in textbooks for projects and references. It's also ideal if you need to find something quickly, such as a specific passage or section. While keeping the lid of the pen on, you read each sentence and 'underline' as you do, effectively completing the task of reading quickly. You may not retain the information as thoroughly at first, though this will improve over time with practice. The goal of this method is to spend no more than one second on each sentence before moving to the next. This may seem difficult at first until you train your eyes to read and absorb each sentence or phrase quickly. In time, this will improve, and you'll find that you can read and understand quickly without much effort, once your mind is trained with practice.

The Scanning Method

Also known as the preview method, scanning refers to quickly skimming a page or article and identifying specific words or groups of words that can be easily used to put together into a theme or concept of what the paragraph is about. Using this technique, you don't have to read each word or sentence completely to understand the nature or theme of what is being written. If you need to slow down briefly to clarify one or two sentences, this can also be done, though the purpose of skimming is to give you the gist of what is being said without having to read each sentence individually. To get started, focus on the first sentence of each paragraph. This will outline the theme or contention of the paragraph. If you are reading something familiar, you may already know what follows, and skimming through the remainder of the paragraph will verify this.

Scanning works by expanding your peripheral vision to all you to take in more words and phrases at a time, which is like the first method of pointing. This involves training your eyes to see more at one time, instead of focusing too much time on just one or two words at a time.

Incorporating the Skills of Speed Reading into Improving Memory

How did these methods work for my son, and how can they be applied to help you? With my son, we practiced these techniques every time he came across any kind of text. These were not limited to what was only required for his schooling, like the required reading list for his English class; the goal is to apply it to text found in the everyday newspaper, or magazine articles when waiting at the doctors, even handed out flyers, etc. We practiced this every time he came across anything with heavy text, so that we it came time to text that mattered for his schooling, he was already well practiced with speed reading the content. With everyday practice, he was able to see the improvement himself – books no longer scared him, he was consuming news feeds regularly, and in turn, he became more knowledgeable in everyday affairs.

Speed reading is a highly valuable skill that will make many aspects of your life easier. Using the skills of speed reading we can apply this to how we associate certain words, objects, and concepts together. This means we can apply visuals to words we see often and apply them to groups or ideas that help us remember the specific items we need to remember. When I combined the skills of speed reading and memorizing with my son, the results came very quick. He was not only able to digest more information faster but was able to remember the information better and more efficiently, which provided a stronger base for building a stronger memory. He developed the ability to recall and retrieve information quickly, without straining himself in the process.

When applying this for yourself, whether it be for your studies or for any research you need to do, apply it the first time you read the text, then go back and apply it a second time. Don't expect to get it right after the first try, as you will need to keep practicing and learn to become comfortable with the material before it starts getting easier. At times you will find that some content is easier to absorb than others. It is only through continual practice that these methods proved to be effective and gave my son a better grasp on the material he was learning, which allowed him to improve his memory skills dramatically. Imagine having the skills to read 2,000 words in one minute instead of 250, and only having to re-read or review sections that are not clearly understood or that you need to become more familiar with. How many books will you begin to read?

How Speed Reading and Visual Memory Patterns Work Together

The various techniques for speed reading may seem different from how memory visuals work to establish a clear pattern in your mind, though they are similar in several ways. Linking visuals such as objects, reminders, and stories to a specific list can create a pattern that may be easier to use as you start to have similar lists to work with. When it comes to reading, you may notice how certain authors favor a specific structure or use certain phrases and word combinations. This can help increase the speed at which you read and digest their books because certain terms and words are used frequently. A certain subject or topic will include a familiar language that will become more predictive and easier to read over time. This creates a mental picture of terminology that repeats in various contexts throughout a book or series of articles or chapters. Consider this example: your mind becomes accustomed to associating pictures or visuals with a list of items, such as a grocery list or art supplies for a project. For a new project, the items may vary but follow the same theme, making them easier to remember with less effort each time. This is because your brain forms new pathways and strengthens the existing neuropathy that is similar to previous lists. When you read one chapter on a book about cats, you'll notice familiar terms used throughout: breeds, feline care, fur, and so on. These and other terms, as well as phrases will change, however, they will remain common and consistent as you progress throughout the book. When this happens, it becomes easier to skim or scan each page. In the example of the book about cats, you'll know right away whether the book's next topic is focused on veterinary care or attributes of certain breeds of cats, as you would have had read plenty of similar style books in the past.

I had a client who was a fan of trains and was eager to learn as much about this topic as he could. So, we applied some of these methods to increase his speed to allow him to absorb the material quicker. The first chapter focused on the history of steam engines, which he initially found interesting, but quickly became bored as he continued its first chapter. This is because the book focused a lot on the dates and times when steam engines were built, how they ran, and their routes, etc. To me, I found it fascinating, because I was able to visualize how each train looked, and the design and shape of its path through towns, countryside, forests, and over bridges. I decided to use this visual to engage my client, which seemed to help a little, but once we physically drew pictures to represent these facts and information, his excitement grew into fascination!

Historical dates, timelines, and date ranges are one of the most difficult things to learn and remember. This is because the information is often presented in a dry and uninteresting format that doesn't stick in our mind. How often have you had to re-read a chapter in a book or textbook with dates to commit them to memory? Chances are, you've done this, only to re-read the text several times. Did you succeed in remembering all the dates and their relevance, even after reviewing the material several times? One of the best ways to imprint a timeline into your mind is to draw an actual line on a sheet of paper in segments and dividing each year or range of time across decades, centuries, and more. For some, a fun technique is to design a board game, where a path begins at the earliest years and progresses from one section or timeframe to the next. Using colors and pictures, this is an effective way to learn dates and times in history. Add images that specifically relate to the era and/or topic that the timeline is about. For trains, my client and I searched for images online, then printed them to cut and paste on a bristle board, which was excellent for affixing several symbols, numbers (years, specific dates) and pictures that would signify the development of trains from their humble beginnings to more sophisticated high-speed travel today. Similarly, you can use a creative picture-based method, such as a calendar or a chart, to create a guide or reference tool to help you remember various dates and events.

Method 3: Fact Association

Fact Association is common to how we remember and make sense of things around us. When we think of the 'beach', we often associate it with water and sand, crashing waves, or the glaring sun on a hot summer's day. When we think of historical events like World War 2, Hitler may come to mind, or the Holocaust or Pearl Harbor. Our memory often depends on these associations to navigate through the various information that we have been presented with over time. Similarly, when we find that we can't remember something, it's often because we cannot find an obvious association with what we need to remember, even though previously we may have been able to.

When we can create associations with the information provided, we can then improve our capacity to remember things more. An effective way to do this is to relate new facts back to something that we already know as opposed to something completely new. This is because what we already know (through various associations to other different facts) is already fixed in our brains, so when we do need to recall it, it is easier to do so. For example, if you needed to learn about theropod dinosaurs, it may be hard to remember that they are flesh-eating dinosaurs when you are new to this group of animals. However, if you have seen the movie Jurassic Park, you could associate theropods to the tyrannosaurus in the movie and recall just how ferocious that animal was. Allow yourself to make associations that work best for you, as your memory and what you've learnt previously can be different to those around you.

Associate with Deep Examination

When we are working with complex facts, data, or even statistics, it may seem impossible to associate these things with anything that we've known previously. However, if we take a step back and try to examine these things thoroughly, even the most complex of facts can be broken down to smaller pieces of information and be made sense of. Examining facts requires that you pull apart information with a series of questions to get your mind thinking about every aspect of the information. When you do so successfully, you will then find it easier to associate the smaller pieces of information to facts that you can work with.

The key to this exercise is to ask questions that excite you and forces you to dissect the information that you are looking at. The traditional *what, when, where, why* and *how* all work, but it's also very important that the questions you use allows you to question the relationship of the information on hand. For example, looking back to World War 2 that we mentioned earlier, if your focus was how World War 2 started, typical questions that you can ask to start the examination process could be:

What year did World War 2 begin?

Who started World War 2 and why?

Who were the Allies and who were the Axis?

These questions are great to kick start the understanding of such a complex history in time; however, what you'll be faced with will just be more information and facts that you need to remember. This is why it's important to ask questions that allow you the ability to relate it to other facts.

If World War 1 ended in 1918, how many years later before World War 2 would begin?

This is especially useful if you have already learnt about World War 1, as you would then be able to leverage off your understanding of the first World War to make your understanding of World War 2 a lot easier. The answer, 21 years, would also be especially easy to remember as this is the age where we would usually associate with a significant milestone in life.

But what if you weren't interested in World War 1? Well then, try and see if you can probe into another event that would help you remember this date better:

What happened 21 years prior to the start of World War 2? The Spanish Flu of 1918.

Deep examining questions can go in any direction you see fit, so long as associations can be made so that the facts make sense to *you*. Not everyone will make the same association of one fact to another, so allow yourself to be creative when doing this extremely effective exercise.

BONUS: Using Acronyms and Acrostics

Something we tend to forget about as we grow older, is how effective acronyms and acrostics work for us when we were a child. Acronyms and acrostics function similarly in that the letters that make up a word are associated individually with another to help us memorize things easier. For example, when we were taught how to spell 'Wednesday', some of you may have remembered the following:

We **E**at **D**onuts **N**early **E**very **S**aturday, **D**onuts **A**re **Y**ummy!

This was an effective way to help spell the word for the longest day of the week, because as kids, we were more inclined to remember it through a rhyme than to recite the letters as is.

As we grow older, rhymes may or may not have the same effect, but creating acronyms to help remember concepts can definitely make challenging things easier to digest. I've taught college students to remember the order of how to complete their work with these methods before. In particular, I remember working with a young woman once who wanted to become a nurse. She was overwhelmed with remembering all of the signs and symptoms of varying conditions. One acronym that she used regularly was for hyperkalemia—the event of having too much potassium in the body. Now, this is a very dangerous condition that can be deadly if left untreated, as potassium is responsible for aiding in the contractions of muscles. What's the most important muscle in the body? The heart! If untreated, hyperkalemia becomes dangerous - *murderous* even. With her, we worked together and found many acronyms that are commonly used in nursing, including one for hyperkalemia: MURDER. This stood for:

- **M**uscle cramps
- **U**rine abnormalities
- **R**espiratory distress
- **D**ecreased cardiac contractility
- **E**KG changes
- **R**eflexes

Morbid? Maybe a little bit—but it definitely helped her to remember the symptoms. In fact, there are many of these used in the medical field, which just goes to show how effective they are. Hypocalcemia was another example, where we found the acronym of CATS: Convulsions, Arrhythmias, Tetany, and Spasms and Stridor. While all of this may be meaningless if you have no real medical background, the ability to aid the young nursing student largely came from these types of patterns. So, start getting creative the next time you find that you're struggling to remember a concept or a spelling. See if you can find a way to associate what you need to learn with an acrostic or acronym and have fun while you're at it!

Method 4: Mind Maps for Complex Matters

The way our brain works is amazing and intricate, often with many details that are recalled subconsciously. A mind map works in much the same way: it is a map or blueprint that analyzes and mirrors how we think. Creating a mind map is both educational and fun. It's a great tool to understand more about how we think and process information, including how we learn. The process of creating mind maps originated many years ago as a way to organize and visualize how our mind and memory work. It's an excellent way to stimulate your brain and its power to form new ideas. Mind mapping can also track progress on a project and give you an opportunity to 'check-in' on how you are improving or expanding on ideas. Consider this process a more powerful way of brainstorming, but with much more to offer.

How are mind maps used in practical scenarios? Many people, young and old whom I've worked with on learning methods, have asked this question. The idea of brainstorming and 'creating' a world in our minds is fun, but how can this solve homework dilemmas and everyday tasks? Some of the most important inventions and machines we use today were built with a mind map, such as computers and aircrafts. By mapping your mind, you can manage the information you require to remember and apply items as needed. When working on a project there are a lot of details involved, which makes it a difficult task to remember everything. Writing these details down will help, but a page full of key terms and highlighted points may not mean anything when you go to look back at a few hours later, or worse, a few days later. Connecting what you write to ensure all points are relevant to each other is what mapping can do for you.

What is the anatomy of a mind map and what do maps consist of? From what you've read so far, mind maps may seem complex, like a detailed and intricate blueprint, but they're actually quite simple so long as you get the core structure right. Consider the following when creating a mind map:

- Start in the center with a core or main topic. As you think on this topic, your mind will expand to consider subtopics or other items that will relate to the core. An arrow or line can be drawn on a paper to illustrate how these various items are connected to the main idea

- To keep the process of mind mapping simple and effective, only one topic or item should be at the core. Other items that relate to the topic will be considered as 'branches' or 'extensions' to the original idea or plan. Essentially you want to focus on the main point and only expand with what's relevant

- If there are subtopics, further branches can provide more specific ideas, keeping in mind that they should be relevant. Consider the following example:

Brand name for restaurant (franchise) -> the main topic
Subtopics (just a few as an example):

  - Franchise locations
  - Menu items and food products available for purchase in stores
  - Marketing and sales

Within each subtopic, like 'franchise location' as an example, there may be further details on the size, building specifications, and whether some locations are smaller 'express' stations and others are full dine-in restaurants. Marketing and sales can expand to include television, internet, and billboard methods for ads, etc.

- Mind maps can be drawn on paper, and this is much more engaging than looking for a compatible computer program or graphics to create online. Drawing your mind map is like a sketch: at first, you'll have a good idea of an outline, then as you fill in the 'shading' or details, you may have to erase or backtrack a few times until you know which items are best to include, and which to omit as irrelevance

- If you are computer savvy, using a program to create a mind map may be your preference. When you were younger, you may have had to create these on large butchers' paper to illustrate your thoughts. As adults, and with all these new technology that is now available to us, there are a lot of programs and software out there that will allow you to use your tablet and laptop to do just the same thing as when you were younger with that large butcher's paper

- Mind mapping is structured, but also widely flexible and with the potential for changing directions and expanding where you least expect it!

In my experience using mind maps, the benefits of planning and stimulating the mind is a major part of the process. Still, there is much more in terms of benefits: slowly you'll begin to feel more confident in your ability to take control of your thoughts and ideas. With practice, you'll be more inclined to express and explore new possibilities that are outside of what you've been used to, allowing you to leave your comfort zone. In this way, better and more improved quality thinking results from this process.

Individual Vs. Group and Other Mind Mapping Possibilities

Creating a mind map is not limited to one person or a set number of people, which means that it is suitable to use even in a workplace setting. When introducing this to your colleagues, assign everyone a section or 'branch' for them to expand on. Imagine in a corporate meeting where a representative from each department is present and ready to give their department the specifications it needs. This cross-team collaboration will only fester more imaginative and innovative ideas compared to traditional methods that you've been accustomed to. If you're assigned a group assignment in school, assign each of your group members a 'branch' based on the individual's strengths or what they feel confident about. This will keep them engaged in the project and allow them to expand their ways of thinking to better contribute to the group's success.

The Benefits of Mind Maps

Outside of their obvious advantage of expanding our minds and thinking process, mind mapping can have many other benefits you may not expect. Mind maps allow you to share and engage with others, where this may not happen in a regular meeting or group setting.

It's a great way to open and express your ideas and become involved with other people: they will learn from you and you from them. If you engage in a group session or lesson online to create a mind map, this can be done effectively with a whiteboard or a similar interactive page to allow you to share ideas and build on them.

What Do You Need to Start a Mind Map?

Great imagination and an open mind are required, which anyone can possess and use to their advantage. We often take for granted how well our minds work, and how we can 'invent' or create new solutions to old problems that may seem unsolvable. We also can learn and retain a lot of information, often beyond what we think, and we can recall facts and ideas that may have been forgotten for some time, only to later find them entering our mind unexpectedly, or when we need it most. When we create a mind map, we enable those ideas, and relevant items remembered to become a part of a plan. This not only helps you to strengthen your memory in the process but also put those memories to practical use.

Aside from having a good imagination, using the power of association is another great way to create a mind map. We may not realize it, but many items in our minds are connected. This is because of previous memories we may have in our life. For example, consider how thinking about a dog as a pet may produce a lot of favorable thoughts if you grew up raising a dog and spent a lot of time playing with them. A project involving pets can allow you to tap into previous memories and ideas you have as a result of connecting with a dog, cat, or household pet. This gives you an advantage not just because of the experience, but your memory of it and how it can be connected or 'mapped' into the current project.

There are many tools to use when creating a mind map, and the more colorful and creative, the better! Tapping into your artistic side, even if you don't think you have one will give you a boost when you unleash your thinking and mindset to consider all possibilities.

We are all capable of creativity, even if we don't think we have a creative bone inside of us. Everyone has a creative side; it just manifests in different ways. While the artistic expression is one of the most obvious signs of creative talent, it is also in the way we communicate, describe, and incorporate new items or ideas into existing plans. It is this way where we can find new solutions that are more effective than previously applied methods.

Chapter 4: Reel in That Focus

Now that you know the four methods to boosting your memory and learning ability, how do you apply them when staying focused can be a challenge? Distractions are often the main culprit for a lack of focus, and these days with the influx of new apps and technologies, it can be quite a challenge for anyone to stay focused on any task they're doing. While limiting distractions can be as easy as removing digital devices and online access for a short period, our minds can often wander away from our task at hand, making it extremely difficult to concentrate. How often have you had to complete something important only to find yourself procrastinating instead? During those times, the task that can take an hour to complete, can often double or triple in the time required, simply because our minds aren't fully focused on the task at hand.

Unlike what you may think, it is not a lack of intellect or innate ability that prevents one from better comprehension and learning. A lack of focus can be a major hurdle for those in completing goals or tasks set for themselves. Some people are able to pay attention even with distractions going on, while others can struggle to maintain their attention span with simplest of tasks. But there are helpful ways to improve focus so that learning becomes easier and less fragmented over time. This will not only enable you to learn and comprehend more effectively, but you will also retain more material at once and for longer periods. What you will need to consider and begin to improve on, is a little thing called self-discipline. With self-discipline, you'll be able to keep yourself on track. Not only will it help improve your focus, with practice it will enable to complete set tasks so that your learning is improved dramatically. As your focus improves, so too does your capacity to learn.

What Is Self-Discipline?

Self-discipline is the ability to take control of your actions and emotions. Working on your self-discipline will give you the ability to develop the self-control needed to help you stay focused and keep you on track. The key to self-discipline is to develop the capacity to forego instant gratification and pleasure, preferring the reward of waiting and gaining more over time. Think of it this way—to have self-discipline is to be able to tell yourself that you will forego that slice of cake because you are on a diet, and you do not want to mess it up. You need to exercise the self-control to tell yourself that you will be happier long-term if you stick to your diet and will be able to enjoy the long-term benefits than if you had the slice of cake. Self-discipline is being able to recognize that short-term, you may be happier if you did something, but knowing that that action will stand in the way of your long-term goals.

Self-discipline, along with willpower, needs to come together to create what you will need in order to take real action. Having the two qualities will help you overcome laziness and unnecessary procrastination, providing you with the power that you will need to keep your focus where it belongs. But self-discipline is also about understanding your progress and being patient with yourself. I often teach my clients that self-discipline is more than just doing what you have to do when you have to do it—it is also taking the time to recognize that you must be patient with yourself when you're doing what you need to do.

With self-discipline, you will understand that the power to take control of your life lies within you. It is empowering—you learn to recognize that even if you feel like you are not making progress, every single step matter on your journey. A fable that I use to illustrate the importance of self-discipline is the one about the tortoise and the hare. In a race where all eyes were on the hare to win, it was the tortoise that came out on top. The tortoise won the race not simply because he kept going, but because he had the self-discipline to continue to take those steps needed to reach the finish line. For the tortoise, it isn't about the speed - it is about the effort and your inner determination – your inner drive.

Something that I tell my clients all the time is this: if it takes you twice as long as someone else to learn the material, you have both technically reached the same spot: you both have attained the same knowledge. Sure, you may have spent longer in obtaining that knowledge, but the fact that you persevered, the fact that you had the self-discipline to continue, is the ultimate difference between success and failure.

Building Self-Discipline

Knowing that self-discipline is the key to your success and to being able to learn effectively, you may wonder what it is that you will have to do to achieve it. You may be wondering how you can build it up to use for yourself, and the answer is simple: self-discipline is crucial to improving your learning and your capacity to learn, but it really is just a series of habits that you will need to build over time. And just like with the example of the tortoise and the hare, progress can be slow at first, but with perseverance, you'll be able to develop the self-discipline you need to achieve those results.

Beginning the Day with Exercise

We all know that physical exercise is important to staying healthy, but regular exercise also plays a significant role in how your mind functions. The routine that comes with regular exercise is the easiest habit you can start working on to building your self-discipline. Athletes will be the first to tell you that their success is not and cannot be achieved overnight. For example, you will never wake up one day from being a couch potato to becoming the next NBA star. The skills an athlete develops over time all comes down to the discipline required to train daily and regularly.

Should you aim to exercise with the same intensity as an athlete? Of course not, though you can if you want to! But like an athlete, know that as soon as you stop exercising, your progress and your chance of success also stops with it.

Try to take on the kinds of exercise that you're most comfortable with. For example, aim to start your day with a 2-minute routine of jumping rope, or go for a 20-minute morning jog. Even something as simple as spending 5 minutes stretching as soon as you wake up. The goal of this is to get yourself to decide on a routine and stick with it. With the health benefits that come with exercise it will make it easier for you to continue with the routine, effectively building the discipline required to maintain this habit. Once you start applying that discipline to your health, you'll notice that your focus will improve, and within the period set out for your exercise routine, distractions would be the last thing on your mind.

Set Goals Each Day to Guide Your Progress

If you dive straight into the task at hand without any prior goals set, you might find yourself losing direction, or forgetting the main purpose of why you started half-way through the task. Setting goals early will allow you to recognize the milestones you've set for yourself, that not only allows you to recognize when you make progress but allows you to feel a sense of accomplishment once you do reach those goal posts.

Goals can be simple. When you read a book, your goal can be to reach a certain chapter before a certain time. When you're writing a thesis, your goal could be to ensure the points you want to address are all addressed by a certain word count. It's important to break down tasks into smaller, more manageable ones, simply because smaller tasks can be easier to achieve. In the example of reading a book, you might be put off by reading something that contained 1000 pages, which would naturally make you not motivated to start at all. However, if you set yourself the goal to read 100 pages each night, or one or two chapters before bed, you'll find that you can finish the book in less than two weeks. Being able to maintain progress every night will allow you to feel the small success early, so that once the book is complete you can then feel the accomplishment you deserve.

Cut out Temptations

If you need to focus on something, it can be hard to resist the temptations of giving in to something else instead. If you need to avoid getting distracted, then you need to remove the things that can tempt you. Just as if you were on a diet, your pantry shouldn't have junk food and snacks to steer you off track. You want to make sure that you are able to keep your eyes on what you want, and that means creating an environment that can allow you to focus. Being able to remove your biggest temptations will be the easiest way to resist temptations. After all, if you don't have easy access to things that steer you off track, are you really going to get distracted?

If you want to avoid losing sight of the task at hand, try putting the phone away. Lock it up somewhere else or leave it out of your room. If you need the phone for phone calls, then make sure to turn off notifications. In fact, try taking a step further and turn off your Wi-Fi entirely. That way you won't be tempted to search for the news or check in to your social media accounts.

Make sure you're also reducing the noise that can take your attention away from what you are doing. Turn off the tv that's going on in the background – why is it on in the first place? If your home has temptations that you cannot remove, then remove yourself entirely from it. Go to the library or go work at your local park or café. Just like being on a diet, your success comes from your ability to walk away from the sweets and the chocolates and the fries. The biggest hurdle will be to walk away from your temptations, but once you do, completing any task will become easier.

Maintain a Steady Sleep Schedule (Even on the Weekends!)

Your body will naturally come to expect things if you have a set schedule. Think about how you feel hungry around midday, no matter the day of the week. You are hungry because your body is used to eating lunch at that time. Likewise, you might find that you are awake at the same time every day, even on the weekends. This is because your body can predict those schedules and will often let you fall into a routine. Make sure you sleep well and go to bed at the same time every night. This will effectively schedule your sleeping pattern so that your body will be conditioned to seep at set times and falling asleep will be less of a challenge. If you are typically a light sleeper and find a full night's rest is not always possible, try meditation and/or light exercise just before sleep. A minimum of seven hours each night is ideal for better focus and alertness the next day. Most of our problems with focus and attention to detail can be resolved simply by getting the hours (and quality) of sleep we need!

Maintaining Your Self-Discipline

When you're deeply engaged in learning, you may be so engrossed in the topic at hand, that the initial purpose or goal of everything you set out to do becomes lost. Once you forget or lose sight of this goal, the challenges of staying on track can become even more difficult. At this stage, it can feel easy to give up or abandon the smaller goals because the initial goal has faded from your mind. You may think this impossible, considering many of us set out to study with a major reason in mind: to obtain good grades, succeed in school, and obtain a steady, profitable, and rewarding career. For those of us already working, further study and goals are needed for career advancement. But even with the clearest idea in mind, encountering several hurdles along the way can make it difficult to focus on the smaller goals, which can get lost in the plan as a whole.

So, what can you do to maintain your focus for the long-term, without losing sight of your smaller tasks, like assignments, and exams? It is easy to feel lost at times, when the amount of reading, studying, and volume of work is high, and some concepts are difficult to understand and apply in your work. This can be overwhelming and frustrating, which makes learning feel more challenging than ever. When this happens, it can make you feel like giving up or postponing the next lesson, which will only prolong or delay what you need to learn and achieve. Maintaining self-discipline can be difficult, but not impossible. It might require some planning to keep yourself on track, but when you do it, you will find those study sessions coming much easier than they were before. Try implementing these small actions that will help you to stick to what you need to do so that you can be certain that you are on track.

Write Down Milestones and Track Your Progress

Just as you started with setting goals for yourself to build on your self-discipline, continuing on this will allow you maintain it. Our minds are positively 'rewarded' or enjoy a sense of reward every time we finish or complete a task, especially if it isn't the easiest. When this happens, we feel the sensation of reward and move onto the next chapter or stage of our mission. By breaking down each stage into smaller components, we not only feel as though more is accomplished, but we also experience the sense of receiving a reward more often, which becomes an incentive to achieve more. By seeing that you are on track, it is easier for you to stick to it as well because you will not want to lose the progress that has been made.

Set Time for Fun

Yes, focus is important, but you also need time to relax. If you find that you constantly end up spending time procrastinating because you have a lot of work to do and you deserve the break before you do begin, you may end up procrastinating so much that you completely fail to achieve what you have set out to do. This can be highly problematic, but the easiest way to navigate through this is setting up a time that is dedicated to relaxing. Maybe you use a certain hour each day just for downtime. You need that to help keep your focus batteries charged. I typically recommend writing out a daily schedule and blocking out a non-negotiable time for fun each day. Use it, even if you feel the temptation to just skip it – the feeling you get after a break will give you more energy to continue with your tasks.

Self-Discipline Activities to Keep You Focused and Motivated

When it comes to maintaining your self-discipline, there are a few activities that I tend to always go back to. If you feel like you need that boost, see if the below helps. From meditating to employing the Pomodoro technique, or even choosing certain sports that require a degree of self-discipline, you can work to ensure that your body and mind are poised to succeed. Each of these different activities can help to prepare you to get into that headspace that you need to focus on what you must get done truly. I've found both activities complement well with each other and the combination of the both generates the most success. For most of my clients, what works well is to get into the right headspace with meditation and then tackling the work with the use of the Pomodoro technique to avoid burning out.

Meditation for Self-Discipline

Meditation is easy to get into once you start forming a routine. Meditation helps you to get into a state of focus in which you are completely aware of what you are doing and how you are doing it. The hustle and bustle of life can make it seem counterintuitive to spend time doing what some may consider 'nothing' to achieve 'anything'. But meditation allows you to regroup and take stock of yourself. It gives you time to really connect with your inner self, and through this activity, you'll be pleased to know that without realizing, you are actively honing and building on that focus and self-discipline.

The first rule to meditation is to first commit time to it. Like establishing any routine, you want to set aside a time that works best for you. My favorite time to meditate is the first thing in the morning. This way, you get to start your day off with meditation, and that will help you to get up and tackle whatever it is that you will have to focus on later in the day. No matter whether you have school, work, or a long day of chores and errands ahead of you, being able to meditate will help you to focus. To make the most of your meditation, make sure you consider the following.

1. *Prepare the environment:* To begin, you want to make sure that you are somewhere quiet and reasonably free from distractions. Make sure that wherever you are is comfortable. Settle comfortably into a chair with your hands in your lap, back straight, and allowing your neck to relax.
2. *Breathing:* Next, you need to breathe. Let your eyes relax and try not to focus on anything. Then, take in five deep breaths - in through the nose and out through the mouth. On the fifth breath, close your eyes.

3. *Focus:* Next, you want to check in with yourself. Pay attention to how you feel, both in mind and body. Look inwards at yourself, starting from your head and down to your toes. Don't be tempted to do anything else when you do this—just note where you feel stressed or tensed. Then, repeat this with emphasis on which parts feel relaxed.
4. *Listen to your thoughts:* As you do this, be mindful of what you think and feel. Don't beat yourself up—just take note of them and become aware. Then, ask yourself why. Why do you feel this way? What do you want to achieve from those feelings?
5. *Focus on your breath:* Then, move on to your breathing. Don't change it—just feel it rising and falling within yourself and how that sensation flows over you.
6. *Wrap up:* When you feel that the time is up - which can be as quick as 5 minutes or as long as 10 minutes – slowly open your eyes and focus back in on the present. Notice how your body feels in the chair and have a

think about what you are about to go out and do. Once you've taken stock of the moment, slowly and calmly get up to get back on with your day.

People tend to forget just how much positivity you can take away from meditation. Not only will you begin the day with a good mood but being more relaxed and 'present' after a meditation session will allow you to enjoy the day ahead of you, which in turn help you yield better results.

The Pomodoro Technique

Another activity that you can use to help you maintain focus is the Pomodoro technique. This is a time management technique that greatly assists with getting through your work. It is named after the Italian word for tomato, thanks to the fact that Francesco Cirillo, who developed this technique, used a tomato-shaped timer to help himself focus in college. He would set his tomato timer and would work in intervals with short breaks. He would work for 25 minutes, then take a 5-minute mental health break. This works well to help you get through your work without feeling burnt out. It makes you more cognizant that while your timer is ticking, you are busy, and you are not allowed to stop working on what you need to do. When the five-minute break arrives, you are then free to do whatever you like.

I've seen positive results from this technique, so I encourage you to try utilizing this yourself—it is incredibly useful when it comes to trying to keep your time management actually manageable. When you are racing against a clock, is easier to maintain your focus if you know that the end (after the 25-minute interval that you've assigned yourself) is within reach. Knowing that you also get a break after that will also give that extra motivation for you to finish the task.

To best use this technique effectively, do the following:

1. Divide the task you need to do into smaller tasks, and list them on a piece of paper or whiteboard, or whatever you have available
2. Start on the first task and set your timer (usually to 25 minutes, but you can use other increments, such as 15 minutes or 45 minutes if you wish)
3. Work on the task
4. Stop when the timer goes off and check off the task on your list. If you have less than four checkmarks, take a 5-minute break and go back to step 2.
5. When you have four checkmarks, take a longer break, between 15 and 30 minutes (typically about the length of your timer intervals) and then reset your count to 0 and go back to task 1.

By implementing this, you may find that you are actually far more receptive to being able to get through these tasks than you originally thought. Give it a shot the next time you need to do something that you don't particularly feel motivated to doing —you may find it easier to stay focused if you can break down the tasks into smaller ones, and checking them off every time one is complete.

Chapter 5: Understanding Distractions and Knowing How to Overcome them

Distractions can occur in any setting and can impact anyone. For some of us, distractions can take up a good chunk of our day, rendering us completely unproductive and can make us feel as if our days were wasted. When thinking of distractions, it is important to recognize what they are and why they impede on our learning. For many, background noise, even in public spaces, can be easy to ignore especially when they are heavily engrossed in what they are doing. For others, this may not be the case as the opposite is true. If we look at distraction as anything that can pull away at our concentration and focus levels, then this can vary from one person or individual to the next. If this is the case, why are some people more distracted than others? And, if you are prone to being distracted often, are there ways to better prepare ourselves to fight these distractions off?

There are a few factors to consider about distractions and why they are so important to any progress we seek. A distraction has the power to control you or your efforts, and when this happens, we lose sight of the task that we are doing. When you lose sight of your task, it becomes a challenge to complete even the simplest of tasks, and you can find yourself spending twice, if not three times more than the original time required. Have you ever tried to finish reading a book that no longer interested you, only to find that your attention has suddenly been turned to the latest T.V show screening? Before you know it, a few days pass and it becomes harder and harder to get back into the book that you've spent every day reading. Or maybe you've been working on a thesis with a looming deadline, but your friend's latest antics compels you to stop 'just for a second' and join them instead? This 'just for a second' ends up taking longer and longer and you may find that you've not met the deadline and are suddenly in all sorts of trouble. We all know to some extent that distractions are caused by boredom, or the lack of interest or attractiveness of the task at hand. Which can be a worry, because not all tasks are able to maintain and rivet our attention in its entirety, so there will bound be times when we will be susceptible to being distracted. Defeating distractions, therefore, is crucial to ensuring that targets for our learning are met, and we are able to achieve the goals that we set out for ourselves.

Six Tips to Eliminating Distractions

Distractions are a reality of life, so it's really all about putting yourself in a better position to 'win' against the distractions that are out there to tempt you. In these times especially, with the prevalence of social media and services that are available at our beck and call, it can be a difficult battle. You'll find that for the majority of times, what you are stacked against is the temptation of convenience and ease, with the road to success too distant to even imagine. Being able to stick with your convictions and having hard resolve can take years to cultivate, but the below tips are immediate solutions that will help you on this journey.

Tip #1

Design or arrange a space where you can study and learn distraction-free as much as possible. If your home has a private office or your bedroom or a den is available for a quiet and peaceful study, make this your 'go-to' spot for learning and reading. Be sure this is a spot or area that you enjoy spending time in so that you feel comfortable when you immerse yourself in books and learning. Include items that will bring comfort and motivation: family photos, vacation photos, plants, a window with natural sunlight, and anything positive. Do not include, or try to avoid things, that can distract you such as a T.V or gaming console.

Tip #2

Turn off your cell phone, and any social media sites on your computer when you read or study. Even if you have the self-discipline to stop using these websites, you'll continually be alerted with notifications or inbox messages, which can be a continuous distraction over time. If you are in a difficult spot of your task, just one notification that you would normally ignore could ignite a conversation, which will allow you a quick escape from the difficulty of the problem you are struggling with. Even when there is sufficient time to break from work, social media should be strictly off the table, and instead, use meditation or exercise, to relieve your stress.

Tip #3
Always start with a goal in mind and make sure to finish the day having met this goal. Earlier we talked about the importance of setting goals and milestones and breaking tasks into smaller, achievable targets. If your goal is to finish reading a chapter every night before bed, then make it happen by not allowing yourself to go to sleep until you finish the chapter. If you find that your goal is simply not achievable, then break it down further into smaller more achievable goals. Maybe you need to reach a certain paragraph within the chapter before you get to sleep? By adjusting your expectations to what is achievable you allow yourself to maintain consistency in finishing each milestone. This will allow you to feel satisfied

and motivated to continue, which results in steady progress.

Tip #4

When you hit a wall with a difficult problem that you can't readily solve, it can be easy to give up and find a distraction from your work. When this occurs, don't cave in! Find an alternative solution or try more than one method. If you are stuck on a concept or problem that you cannot resolve on your own, make sure you have some resources handy to reference. Tutorial videos that specifically relate to what you're working on, or a colleague, family member, or friend can sometimes be of help when you need it most. Sometimes it's not about whether or not you can solve a problem or understand a lesson, but stagnant progress over time can cause you to lose interest, especially if you've been working on it for a while. Don't let this distract you from finishing your goal, even if it is just one lesson or a portion of it.

Tip #5

Allow yourself to be awarded anytime you achieve a milestone. This can be a treat from the kitchen or a top-up of your favorite drink. Little rewards or a 'pat on the back' can go a long way to conditioning yourself to achieve more in the long term. Take an extra five-minute break or go for a walk to enjoy the fresh air outside, so that you feel refreshed and ready to dive back into your work right after.

Tip #6
Sometimes, distraction comes from within and may involve a recurring thought or pattern of thinking that places a limit on your ability to focus on studying effectively. When this happens, it can feel as if you are sabotaging your own efforts to success. Know though, that simply being aware of its presence and making an active effort to put certain ideas or thoughts out of your mind, you can make a difference in getting the most out of your learning. If the recurring thought is emotional, it may be more difficult to control and may require more support and time to relax. When this happens, meditation and mindfulness can make a significant difference. If you can begin your next task

or learning on a positive note, where there are no internal battles to distract you, this can be a quick, yet unexpected way to get the learning you need at a time when your mind is fresh, positive and ready. Handling internal emotional and deeply personal distractions can be a struggle, but with the right support and focus, they can be overcome, and you'll see progress unfold as a result. Remember to allow yourself to visualize your success and see within yourself the power to achieve and make a difference. We often think that what we need to learn better and faster exists outside of us, when a lot of it is on the inside and requires you to tap into this to succeed.

The Myth with Multitasking

People who multitask will say that they do so so that they can get more done in less time. The truth, however, is that more often than not, multitasking only makes you spend longer to complete those tasks. Have you ever tried watching the news as you work on a project or thesis? If you have, how successful were you in retaining all the key facts the news presented *and* completed the project. How about playing an instrument as you read a book? The reality is, not only does multitasking take you longer to complete tasks, you're also more prone to being distracted as you do so.

Studies have shown that when multitasking, you struggle to pay attention, recall information, or switch from task to task. If you think that you can watch a show or text your friend while you work on writing that report, think again. Multitasking is less productive than if you had been able to go from one task to the next without jumping around. It reduces your efficiency because the human brain is only capable of focusing on one thing at a time. Because of this, when you start to multitask, you actually split up that focus, which actually means that neither task you're doing gets the attention that is needed to complete it.

Additionally, it has been found that multitasking can actually cause long-term damage to your brain. In particular, those who spend time on multiple devices are found to have less brain density in the anterior cingulate cortex. This part of the brain is responsible for controlling both cognitive and emotional functions. When you watch TV and text, for example, and sustain that habit over long periods of time, the changes in your brain can be more permanent than you think. You don't just get full functionality back when you turn off the devices—there are lasting changes that, although are gradual, can have lasting detrimental effects on you.

I remember the first time I advised against this with my son. "But why can't I stay on the phone with my friend, dad? I can talk to him and do my math homework at the same time. It's not hard." I laughed at him and decided to make a bet that he wouldn't be able to do it, or if he did, he wouldn't be able to get all the answers right. He took on the bet, as we had already gone through the math questions earlier and he had complained that it was too easy. What resulted? Well, he managed to get all his answers right. But my son later confessed that he was so focused on ensuring that his math questions were right, that he didn't even realize his friend had hung up on him because he had stopped talking on the phone, so deep in his concentration.

It's an amusing story I always recall when someone raises the multitasking debate with me. The reality is everything that that we do requires time and focus. And to do them properly requires our full attention. When we talk about limiting distractions by creating an environment that best allows us to succeed, multitasking is only another form of distraction that pulls away at our ability to focus wholly on a set task. Effectively you are splitting and stretching your attention thin over the number of tasks you choose to take on. So, the next time you're thinking of multitasking, well really, think again.

Managing Addictions that Distract You

It's a strange time we live in with technology and social media permeating every aspect of our life. When I was younger, I remember standing by the radio with a cassette tape on hand, ready to record a hit song so that I could play it on my Walkman later. Nowadays, all you need to do is do a search on YouTube or another music platform, and the song you like is there for you to play on loop. Everything is conveniently placed for us. Technology has really changed our lives dramatically.

Over the years, starting with the sole purpose of working with my son to improve how he learned, to becoming excited with my findings so much so that I began sharing it with others, both young and old, I started to see a different impact technology has on us. Gone seems to be the days where you can easily find yourself immersed in a book or movie of your choosing. The dilemmas I now hear are those who just simply cannot get themselves *interested*. Instead, what takes up most of their time is this little thing called social media.

They explain it like this:

> *"I try to set aside time to read, but I just can never find myself getting into the books that I choose. It's like they're interesting for a bit, but then I just get...bored."*

> *"So, what doesn't get you bored? What do you find yourself doing most of the times?"*

> *"Well I'm on my phone a lot."*

> *"What do you do on your phone?"*

> *"I just look at...stuff. Don't get me wrong, it's not all interesting, but I just... keep looking. It's just always with me and on."*

It's a new type of addiction that has come from the plethora of gadgets and apps that are available online.

And it made me cognizant of a different type of factor that contributes to our distractions: the over-saturation of information that surrounds us. In our current society, we have everything we need to know and learn about at our disposal online. A simple search can reel in thousands of articles, even scholarly and peer-reviewed papers, that provide us with more knowledge and information at once than ever before. When we add this to our use of social media – where everything is the latest, most current, most popular – our thirst for information becomes harder to satiate. What *can* be more interesting than the latest most up-to-date trend? What *better* than to watch the newest video that's just uploaded? Why *wouldn't* we be reading up on emerging research that is happening *right* this instant? The constant dopamine hits we get from satisfying our short-term curiosity begins to numb our ability to seek pleasure in things that cannot be produced immediately. This new addiction that we are seeing, effectively, is changing the way our brain functions.

With addiction, it isn't the immediate effects that is concerning. When you hit that 'refresh' button on your app, or when you can't help yourself from running a search on a new trend, it's easy to say that you will just stop that action to curb your activity. The impacts of social media, much like other addictions, can have drastic consequences long term. When your senses are numb to the pleasures of seeking reward because so much information can be rewarded to you almost instantaneously, it makes other activities that cannot generate the same immediate output far less interesting. Remaining focused on the task becomes a challenge, maintaining any interest seems unlikely, and motivation is ultimately lost. So, when we talk about social media being a distraction, it is beyond just wasting time on a certain app, or having focus temporarily lost. It's important to understand how addiction works in the long term, so that there is greater reason to manage them. So, the next time you look at your phone during your 'breaks', or when you decide against turning off notifications because it isn't 'such a big deal', think about the long-term detrimental impacts it has to your learning as a whole.

Switch it off, and kill not only that addiction, but any chance of it changing the way you learn.

Chapter 6: Habits to Keep

When you develop a plan of learning and improving your memory, you'll likely form new habits to replace what you've done before. Forming habits that impact our external surroundings are important, but so too are habits that impact our inner being. This includes what we eat, how we think and how we move. To understand how your inner health affects the way you learn and how quickly you can absorb information, we need to look at how the brain, physically, works.

Your memories and the information you acquire are stored in the hippocampus part of the brain, which acts as a hard drive or storage place. These two organs are located in the medial temporal lobe and form a part of your body's limbic system, which also regulates emotions. When you acquire new information or learn something for the first time, a new and unique neural pathway is formed. Once formed you will 'revisit' this path as you read and learn more about this new subject, which will strengthen and reinforce this new pathway so that it becomes easier to retrieve or recall information. This is especially helpful during a quiz or an exam. By actively learning and engaging in new material, while building on what you already know, you're strengthening your neural pathways over time.

It's not always about learning something new that creates a stronger neural pathway and memory system in your brain, but how you learn as well. By trying various methods or games to approach problem-solving from different angles, you'll find new and interesting ways to resolve issues that may not have been considered previously. The hippocampus plays a central role that not only builds and expands for the storage of information and expansion of memory, it also allows us to connect various components of our life experience, learning, and memories, including emotional experiences, into our own story of life. For this reason, it is important to take brain health seriously. As the proper function of the hippocampus is required for literally every function we need, from vocalizing our thoughts or recalling specific details to a series of events, and forming new information based on an assessment of what we already know or have stored in our mind.

When the hippocampus is impaired or damaged, it can lead to difficulties in learning and recalling information that we have stored. It may distort what we already know, as the structure of this part of the brain must be intact and in good, functioning order to work well. Several factors contribute to structural damage in the hippocampus, including PTSD (post-traumatic stress disorder), excessive alcohol, memory and cognitive diseases such as Alzheimer's and dementia, and lack of development from conditions such as bipolar depression and schizophrenia. Fortunately, with the right medical treatment and support, there have been many improvements and benefits for individuals who suffer from one or more of these conditions. For example, damage from excessive alcohol consumption, when stopped completely, can be fully reversed in less than one year. Some forms of antidepressants and related treatments have been found to rebuild the hippocampus in the mind of people who suffer from depression. While there is more research needed, along with the development of more solutions to improving the hippocampus' function, there is a lot of positive activity in this field. Many people who have felt they could never learn or develop skills can do so more effectively than ever, thanks to modern science and ongoing research.

Mental and physical exercises combined can create a beneficial wellness plan that can benefit everyone. From someone already at the top of their game, looking to enhance brain function more, to individuals who suffer from a wide range of neurological and mental health disorders. There is a lot to gain from simple exercises, stress management, and using your spare time to enjoy a puzzle or two to stimulate the mind. The more you utilize these activities, in addition to medical treatment and support, you'll find that your memory and ability to build and retain new information and memories become stronger and easier than ever before.

How you learn and the methods you apply can have a profound impact on your brain's function and how well you retain and utilize the information you learn. Keeping your mind healthy is one of the top essentials for productive learning and application in daily life. Without a strong, healthy mind and memory, any attempt at studying or reading will be thwarted as a result because your mind and memory will not be primed to convert short-term memories to long-term storage. Your short-term memory will function well when your long-term memory is strong. To ensure that you have a healthy, long-term memory, it's important to focus on wellness and apply as many preventative measures as possible to avoid memory loss and cognitive impairment. One of the most important aspects of improving and establishing a good memory is keeping up with good habits that will help you to keep your body and mind both in tip-top condition. It is imperative that if you want to be healthy, you need to give your body the right fighting chance to keep itself healthy.

The habits that I always recommend to others to change their lifestyle to be healthier involves three key points: Exercising the body, exercising the mind, and supporting both the body and mind with the right diet to keep your body healthy and strong. If you can follow those key points, you will be in tip-top condition for the most effective learning. There is a reason that so many people try to eat a meal of fish before a big test (to support the brain!) or why it is universally recommended that you exercise regularly.

Exercising the Body to Strengthen Learning

When you get moving, you get the blood pumping throughout your body. As the blood pumps and circulation improves, it also goes up to your brain as well. Of course, your brain needs oxygen so that it can focus and function as well and if you are able to give your brain that boost of energy that it needs, you'll realize that you are actually able to get improvement in that focus that you were looking for. I saw a noted improvement in my son's ability to focus after he exercised, and I think that there were a few key reasons for this. He was able to get that blood pumping, sure, but he also got that excess energy out of his system so that he could focus to his fullest extent. I've seen him struggle with restlessness as he tried to study or learn something, and I've seen it in other children and adults as well. Children typically are not very good at hiding their fidgeting, but the adults tend to show their energy in other ways—they tap their feet or their fingers. They may fiddle with a pen or their hair. Their energy is released one way or another, even if that means through moving around in these ways. In particular, there are six key ways that exercise can help the brain to perform better, and each one is a compelling reason to exercise daily.

Exercise Increases Energy

The more that you move around, the more energy that you develop—the good kind. Through regularly exercising your body boosts your muscles and endurance, as well as having the ability to manage learning of new ideas. Even just 15 minutes of exercise, or even just moving around, will trigger your body to develop more energy used to focus.

Exercise Boosts Focus

After exercising, you will have a two or three hour period that your focus will be elevated. This is thanks to the oxygen that pumps through the body as you exercise that will help you to ensure that you have the energy to keep your mind sharper. Think about how tough it can get to put together a coherent thought when you are exhausted and trying to avoid falling asleep—you eliminate this problem by exercising and waking your body up. I always recommend that before a test or interview, or some other activity that will require intensive focus that my clients exercise. For those who don't like to exercise or tend to associate exercising with running laps, I always recommend smaller activities fit for one's lounge room or backyard. Things like, skipping for one/two minutes, doing 50 squats, etc., anything that can get your blood pumping even slightly, will be able to bolster your focus levels, compared to no exercise at all.

Exercise Enhances Mood

Focus is difficult if you are not in the mood for it. This is just natural—why would you be in the right state of mind if you are upset about something? Thankfully, however, exercise boosts the mood. It releases endorphins, which work twofold to help support your ability to learn. On the one hand, it has been shown that endorphins will elevate your mood. You will have serotonin released into your brain as well during exercise, which is known as the 'happy' chemical. Exercise has been shown in studies to be an excellent mood enhancer for those who need it. Additionally, endorphins have also been linked to better memory as well, which means that you are more likely to remember more after an exercise session.

Exercise Helps with Impulse Control

If you exercise on the regular, you will find that you are actually able to control yourself better as well. That's right—exercise will help to improve your brain's ability to function by improving the prioritizing functions, which are there to determine what to do and when to do it. This means that you are more likely to be aware of when you are being faced with distractions and will have the ability to prioritize the task before you, effectively resisting falling for the mistake of pursuing them. You will be capable of bettering your focus because you will have better self-control.

Exercise Improves Memory

It has been found, according to a study published in the American College of Sports Medicine, that students were able to memorize more if they were physically active. In particular, the students were asked to memorize a list of letters. It was found that the students that ran after reading the list were actually quicker and better at reciting back those letters compared to those who either lifted weights or remained where they sat. Being active helps the body and the mind and will help you immensely when it comes to learning.

Exercise Increases Productivity

Studies have also shown that when you exercise more, you are more likely to be more productive in other aspects in your life. Productivity is one of those areas where, once you start to develop it, it will spill into other aspects of your life as well. You don't have to be a sports star—but if you are more active and find the time to exercise regularly, you will be more productive in just about every other aspect. If you want that productivity rate to go up, you want to get moving.

How Much Exercise Do I Need?

You do not have to live at the gym if you want these benefits for yourself, either—it has been found that even just 30 minutes of elevating your heart rate several days per week will do wonders in improving your ability to function. Current recommendations are that adults need at least 150 minutes of moderate exercise, or 75 minutes of vigorous exercise per week, along with general activity. You can get this with 30 minutes of moderate-intensity cardio five days per week, or you can get it from three sessions of 25-minute vigorous sessions. This will get that blood pumping and boost your mood so that you know that you will be on track for success in learning.

Exercising the Mind to Strengthen Learning

Along with exercising your body, it's important to exercise your brain also, so that you can keep your brain in shape. Find time to challenge your mind with regular activities that allows your brain to think. A lot of activities designed for the brain are hobby-forming, meaning that you can integrate these with your daily lifestyle.

If you want to exercise your mind to ensure that it is working in tip-top condition, think about adding some of the below activities:

- *Word puzzles:* Crossword puzzles and word games are an excellent way to 'warm up' your brain and stimulate the thinking process while creating new neural pathways between nerve cells. The more crossword puzzles you complete, the more associations you make with words, both old and new. This will help expand your vocabulary and deepen your understanding of words and their antonyms (opposites) and synonyms (words with similar meaning).

- *Number games:* Games involving numbers, such as the Sudoku exercise, or equations that use pictures and numbers to solve a puzzle, can be fun when you start getting used to them. Like crosswords, number games (which may include both numbers and words, depending on the type of game), can strengthen your brain's relationship and understanding of how they work. For example, an individual who may not consider themselves to be mathematically inclined may find a puzzle involving numbers less stressful and intimidating. This can help break down any mental barriers to learning more about math, as you begin to feel more comfortable working with numbers.

- *Video games:* Surprised? Online games are not only fun but can build your brain's power to react quickly and problem-solve more effectively. Some specific apps and games are designed for this benefit, and to improve your brain's ability to learn faster, react quickly, and increase your attention span. The speed at which you learn new information and incorporate it into your learning is also improved.
- *Brain teasers:* Learning and writing poems or deciphering riddles or similar puzzles can be an effective way to retrieve and learn new connections between words, numbers, images, and concepts. Some workplaces use brain teasers to break the ice socially while engaging employees to use their brains to 'think outside the box' or to get creative with new ideas and concepts, which generally leads to innovative planning and succession in business. A simple puzzle can make a major difference in how our

brain works, and the more often we apply these skills, the stronger they become.

- *Logic games:* Try traditional games and methods of learning and using logic. Chess and checkers are classic examples of giving your brain the ultimate workout. Not only must you figure out which move to make next, but also factor how your move will impact the next 3-4 moves, and beyond. Chess is one of the most enjoyable, yet complex ways to expand your mind, and enable you to not only react quickly to solve a problem but take into account how your specific move will impact others.

- *The route less traveled:* When driving, cycling, or walking home from work or school, consider taking a new route. Discovering new routes or ways to get from one point to another is an easy way to form new neural paths in your mind, which is important for mental stimulation. When you use the same route over and over again, it puts your mind into autopilot mode, and you don't have to work as hard mentally to achieve the result. By choosing a different route or varying the directions you take from one point to another, you'll expand and stimulate the hippocampus to better expand your brain's ability to build new pathways and learn more.

- *Breathing exercises:* Breathing exercises and slowing down your mind and body is essential to maintaining a balance between the fast-paced world of learning, working, and constantly absorbing new information and giving our mind and body the rest it needs to rejuvenate and replenish. Without taking the time to breathe deeply and slow down for a few minutes, we may not be getting all the oxygen in our brain that we need to function. This can severely limit the hippocampus, which is highly vascularized and needs a lot of oxygen to function effectively.

Eating to Support the Body and Mind

The foods we eat have a major impact on our brain's function and cognitive ability. Following a balanced, nutritious diet is therefore vital for learning success. This is widely supported by doctors, dieticians, and professional educators. Within a balanced way of eating are key foods that boost our brain's power and will make a significant impact on how we perform. While including whole, healthy food options in your diet, it's also important to avoid processed and refined foods that offer little or no vitamins, minerals, or nutrients to support your mind and body. Many will make the mistake of not including their eating habits as a possible culprit for lack of attention, memory challenges, and other hurdles for learning effectively. By making good choices for our diet, we can make a difference simply by how and what we eat.

Key Foods to Include in Your Diet

The following foods are best for cognitive function, memory, and boost your learning potential because they contain a wide range of vitamins (including antioxidants), minerals, protein, and healthy fats, which the brain needs as the foods to help you thrive and function at its optimal level:

- *Fish and Seafood:* The top food for brain health is seafood. It is often referred to as 'brain food' because of its superior level of healthy fats and protein. Salmon, tuna, mackerel, and sardines are among the best options, though there are many types of seafood to include in your diet with various nutrients and benefits for your health. If you're not too keen on fish but would like to introduce it into your diet, try mild-tasting options first, such as salmon, and tuna, which are most commonly added to sandwiches, salads. Then, once you're feeling adventurous, try the popular Japanese plate of sushi. Fish contain omega 3s and protein, along with antioxidants and trace minerals that support brain development and health.
- *Avocado:* This is an excellent option for vegans and those on plant-based diets. Many people enjoy avocado on sandwiches, such as the

popular avocado toast or as a sushi ingredient. Guacamole is a popular dip that works well as a side or condiment. On its own, avocado can be a great snack, but you will find it works best when added to salads or a topping on stir-fries or a wrap. Avocados are full of fiber, vitamins, and healthy fats. When looking for an alternative to fish, especially for those on plant-based diets, avocado is a great option for the number of natural fats it contains. Just two or three avocados a day can have a major positive impact on your health, which is why it is recommend as a healthy part of any diet.

- *Nuts and Seeds:* Nuts and seeds are a great source of healthy fats, fiber, minerals, and other antioxidants. Sunflower, chia, hemp, and flax seeds are among the best to include in your diet and can easily be added to cereals (both hot and cold), homemade granola bars, and other recipes. Chia seeds are one of the most nutrient-rich foods on the planet. They can be added to smoothies, puddings, and cereals to boost you and your family's health. Other seeds, such as sunflower seeds, can also make as a great snack. Walnuts, almonds, pecans, and macadamia nuts are great options for healthy fats and fiber. Both nuts and seeds are easy to add in place of less healthy options, such as candy bars, pretzels, potato chips, and other highly refined sugar and snacks out there.

- *Dark Green Vegetables:* Any raw, fresh vegetables are recommended, but dark, leafy greens are often the best choice for vitamins and iron. One of the most common deficiencies is iron, which can affect the way we perform mentally. By making sure you include a serving of spinach or kale in your meal, you will have the benefits of many nutrients at once. If you're a picky eater and not used to eating dark greens, try adding them on some homemade pizza or in an omelet to mask the taste with the flavors that you like.

- *Yoghurt:* Dairy products are a great way to increase calcium and protein in your diet, and yoghurt is one of the most nutritious options available. If you want to increase the benefits of this food, choose a plain style of yogurt and add your berries, granola, and natural sweeteners, such as honey or maple syrup. This can be a balanced snack option when you need a break and are craving for some food.

- *Eggs:* Omega 3s, protein, and vitamin E are the major highlights of eggs. It is a breakfast staple that can be enjoyed on their own or with a wide variety of foods. The protein and fats in eggs provide an excellent source of fuel for your brain. Not only are eggs simple to prepare, but they are also delicious and can be enjoyed by everyone. Eggs are also excellent in salads and sandwiches.

- *Herbs and Supplements for Optimal Brain Function:* If you decide to take supplements or natural herbs that are known for their brain-boosting ability, always check with a doctor or medical professional to ensure they are safe and beneficial for you. While most natural supplements and herbs are safe, it's recommended that you check first, in case of allergies or other reactions to medication or medical conditions. Some of the following options I've personally found to have worked, as they are proven to be beneficial for brain health and cognitive performance. But again, before you consume these, make sure to consult your doctor:

- *Gingko Biloba:* This a bitter-tasting herb that can be used in its dried form to create a tea, though most people prefer to take this herb in capsule form. Gingko Biloba has been shown to increase blood flow to the brain, including smaller capillaries that may not get the circulation needed.
- *Ginseng:* A potent supplement, ginseng is used to increase energy, and this has an amazing effect on your mind's function too. Ginseng is strong in taste, and it is often combined with other herbs or foods, such as green tea or ginger. Ginseng can also be added to your favorite drink (hot or cold

beverage) in liquid form to minimize the taste.
- *Green tea:* High in antioxidants and among one of the healthiest drinks on the planet, because it contains more vitamins and antioxidants than most fruits and vegetables! There is caffeine in green tea, though it isn't harmful and can help stimulate your mind. There are several varieties of green tea, and recently have been found popular in desserts. Matcha, is an ingredient that is widely used in desserts like cake, brulee and tarts. It's available in powder form and can also be added to a smoothie or a milkshake.

Unhealthy Foods to Avoid for Improving Brain Health

Unfortunately, if there's food that's good for you, there's always food that isn't so good for you. In general, it is best to avoid or skip processed foods completely, as they are not worth the cost and effort, even if they are enjoyable. On occasion, you can enjoy a few potato chips, an ice-cream or a candy bar, just remember that these foods should not become a regular part of your diet.

- *Deep-fried foods:* French fries, onion rings, and other deep-fried foods are best to avoid at all costs because they contain trans fats, which harm health, and have been shown to increase the risk of cancer, heart disease, and can have an ill impact on your brain's function as well. What is the best option for avoiding deep-fried foods? Consider a salad or a baked potato as an alternative. Baked, grilled, and steamed foods contain less trans fats and are not as dangerous and can provide more vitamins and better quality for your meals. Try to avoid fast food as a habit, and if you do make it an occasional treat, just remember that there are many great healthy options available at most food outlets.

- *Soda and High Sugar Drinks:* Fruit juice and soda should be avoided as it contains far more sugar than vitamins. It's common to include juice boxes, and diet soda in lunches or as a part of a meal because often we don't consider the hidden ingredients or sugars that can impact our health. Try replacing these drinks with freshly squeezed homemade juice, sparkling water, or unsweetened tea. It can take a while to adjust to drinking healthier beverages, but it is a worthwhile change that can make a significant improvement.
- *Refined Grains and Pasta:* Carbohydrates are an important part of one's diet, but the wrong types of carbohydrates especially found in refined foods that have low nutrient value are best to be avoided. They may provide short bursts of energy, much like a sugar rush, but can quickly lower your learning endurance and harm processing information. Many of these foods are also high in sugar, which is another reason to avoid them. Choose whole-grain cereals and granola bars as an alternative, as

these foods will give you a good source of steady energy.

Generally, the more fresh, wholesome foods that you put into your body, the better the outcome in learning and brain performance. Always keep in mind that what you eat will impact your brain health. I recommend always keeping a good number of options available at home, including natural snacks and fresh fruits and vegetables, which will naturally steer you away from temptations. Don't underestimate how strong the temptation can be for junk food when you are hungry, and you are faced with no options in your pantry! I know that personally, after a long day's work, the last thing I want to do is go to the shops to buy ingredients for a healthy meal when the local takeout is so much easier!

Eating healthy and exercising regularly is indeed a lifestyle change but is a change where you'll see results immediately. How often have you felt alert and full of energy after eating a heavy meal of take-out food? I would hazard a guess that you never do, instead you'll feel sluggish, sometimes sleepy, and end up being unproductive. Look, we've all been there before so there's no judgement at all! On the contrary, if you eat a plate full of vegetables and lean meat, and swap that packet of chips with some fruit, you'll find that you'll have much more energy to slide back into that book or finish that project or continue that lesson. These immediate changes will allow you to push yourself further along this journey of learning. As they say, small habits make big progress.

My son who struggled with studying and always felt that he couldn't live up to his full potential, always complained that he simply didn't have the energy to learn. By working on a plan to include into his routine good eating habits and daily exercise, both physically and mentally, it would change him completely. I saw a marked difference in his energy output and enthusiasm with learning. It was night and day how much better his mind worked when his body was healthy, and I can be honest to say that even I felt the difference in myself as I joined him in his efforts. I saw first-hand just how important it became for him to have that good, well-balanced diet and get that active time in, and ever since that point, I would always recommend this to everyone I worked with. And that is why I encourage you to try this yourself and see for yourself how quickly you'll see the effects of this change.

Where to Now?

Now that you have the tools, information, and methods to understand how to improve your learning ability, it's vital to put these new skills into practice right away! You are in full control of your learning journey, and these methods will ensure that you experience the fun and joys of learning like never before. Consider all the key factors you'll need to follow to make your learning experience more impactful so that you can avoid the pitfalls of procrastination while enhancing your mind's ability to absorb and comprehend any material thrown at you:

- Have a positive mindset. The journey of learning can go through many challenges and sometimes giving up may feel like the easiest option. Always remember why you started, and what you want to achieve. Daily affirmations will help you to go easy on yourself whenever you hit a roadblock to ensure that you will continue with the mindset to persevere through

- Keep your learning habits regular, even if in short sessions, so that you are always engaged and don't allow yourself the opportunity to be bored. Make your lessons interesting. If it gets boring, it's time to take a break and look to one or more of the new and engaging methods from this book

- Use visual methods, codes, stories and fact association to link objects or items together in your lessons, so that they make sense when you need to recall them for assignments and exams. This will not only help you to strengthen your memory but also improve your understanding of the material in a fun and creative way

- Apply the simple, yet effective, tools of speed reading to learning in a way that allows you to grasp the main concept or idea first, then fill in the details later. When it is determined that some of the material is already learned or understood from a previous lesson, you'll have the opportunity to skip these section(s) and focus only on what's relevant and necessary

- Take control of your learning environment. Ensure that you are working in an environment that allows you to succeed. Recognize when distractions will hit and prepare measures to reduce or eliminate them. Turn off notifications, move away from noise and other distractions if it is not conducive to your learning

- Make sure to look after your health. A healthy mind begins with a healthy body, and this means taking notice of what you consume and how often you exercise. Avoid food that is heavily processed and/or high in saturated fats and refined sugars. When exercising, remember that mental exercises are just as important as physical exercises. Mind health can deteriorate much like physical health if neglected!

Trust in these proven learning strategies and see for yourself the results over time. You've embarked on this journey the moment you've purchased this book, so it's now up to you to continue on this journey to see just how successful these methods can be. Once you see the results, you'll be eager to share them with friends and family. Keep in mind that many others will benefit from these methods of learning, so if you have enjoyed this book, please leave a review on Amazon! By leaving a review on Amazon for this book, you'll be making a significant impact by giving others a chance to apply new and innovative ways to learning and allow them to see the benefits from these techniques that will be life changing. I wish you a wonderful learning journey, as I am confident that from this moment onwards, you have all the tools and knowledge to take full control of your learning, and start learning anything you want, whenever you want!

Resources

Barile, N. (2018, January 16). Exercise and the Brain: How Fitness Impacts Learning. Retrieved August 29, 2020, from https://www.wgu.edu/heyteach/article/exercise-and-brain-how-fitness-impacts-learning1801.html

Bates, T. (n.d.). How to Mind Map: 7 Easy Steps to Master Mind Mapping Techniques, Note-taking, Creative Thinking & Brainstorming Skills. Retrieved August 29, 2020, from https://books.google.com.au/books?id=G0DHDwAAQBAJ

Bradberry, T. (2015, January 20). Multitasking Damages Your Brain and Career, New Studies Suggest. Retrieved August 29, 2020, from https://www.forbes.com/sites/travisbradberry/2014/10/08/multitasking-damages-your-brain-and-career-new-studies-suggest/

DEFEAT DISTRACTIONS WITH THESE 7 TIPS. (n.d.). Retrieved August 29, 2020, from https://kwiklearning.com/kwik-tips/defeat-distractions-with-these-7-tips/

Ergun, E. (2020, January 23). 9 tips to stop multitasking immediately. Retrieved August 29, 2020, from https://www.jotform.com/blog/tips-to-stop-multitasking/

Frey, C. (2018, April 04). 10 outrageously valuable benefits of brainstorming tools. Retrieved August 29, 2020, from https://medium.com/@chuckfrey/10-outrageously-valuable-benefits-of-brainstorming-tools-a9c5e0d06969

Henry, A. (2019, July 12). Productivity 101: An Introduction to The Pomodoro Technique. Retrieved August 29, 2020, from https://lifehacker.com/productivity-101-a-primer-to-the-pomodoro-technique-1598992730

Hill, A. (n.d.). 16 Superfoods That Are Worthy of the Title. Retrieved August 29, 2020, from https://www.healthline.com/nutrition/true-superfoods

Mandl, E. (2018, January 28). The 7 Worst Foods for Your Brain. Retrieved August 29, 2020, from https://www.healthline.com/nutrition/worst-foods-for-your-brain

Morin, A. (2019, October 04). 8 Working Memory Boosters. Retrieved August 29, 2020, from https://www.understood.org/en/school-learning/learning-at-home/homework-study-skills/8-working-memory-boosters

Patel, D. (2019, May 14). 10 Powerful Ways to Master Self-Discipline. Retrieved August 29, 2020, from https://www.entrepreneur.com/article/287005

Staff, M., Smookler, E., Choice, C., Salzberg, S., Booker, L., & Hurlock, H. (2020, August 10). How to

Meditate. Retrieved August 29, 2020, from https://www.mindful.org/how-to-meditate/

Tracy, B. (n.d.). Motivation (The Brian Tracy Success Library). Retrieved August 29, 2020, from https://www.oreilly.com/library/view/motivation-the-brian/9780814433119/xhtml/h3_id_78.html

Manufactured by Amazon.ca
Acheson, AB